134752

# REBUILDING
# THE WALLS

# REBUILDING THE WALLS

## A Biblical Strategy for Restoring America's Greatness

Peter Waldron
with George Grant

Wolgemuth & Hyatt, Publishers, Inc.
Brentwood, Tennessee

Unless otherwise noted, all Scripture quotations are either
the author's own, or are from the New King James Version
of the Bible, copyrighted 1984 by Thomas Nelson, Inc.,
Nashville, Tennessee.

Published by Wolgemuth & Hyatt, Publishers, Inc.
P.O. Box 1941, Brentwood, Tennessee 37027.

Printed in the United States of America.

ISBN 0-943497-04-3

To my beloved wife Pamela
and to my delightful children,
Aaron, Sarah, and Levi

# CONTENTS

# ACKNOWLEDGEMENTS

Many many people have graciously and sacrificially contributed to this project and to the Contact America ministry. I would especially like to thank Melody Blake and the entire Contact America staff for their faithfulness and diligence. I would also like to express my gratitude to Dr. Edwin Louis Cole for the tremendous influence he has had on my life. That this book exists at all is due in great part to the support and encouragement of Mike and Gail Hyatt and Robert and Bobbie Wolgemuth. To them, and to all the other "thinking Christians" who have believed in me and in the message God has given me, I owe a debt I cannot possibly hope to repay. In addition, I would like to offer my sincerest thanks to George Grant. His encouragement, enthusiasm, courage, wisdom, and extraordinary skills are what made this book what it is. Finally, I must say thanks to my mother and father and the rest of my family for all the years that they not only put up with me, but loved me as well.

# INTRODUCTION

There was a time — not too terribly long ago — when America was a *great* nation. Its power, prestige, and prosperity were unparalleled. Its glory loomed over international affairs like a great eagle over troubled waters.

But that time has now passed. A terrible malaise has stripped America of much of its grandeur. The land of the free and the home of the brave still stands tall in the community of nations. But its reputation is undeniably tarnished. Its strength is undeniably diminished.

The decline in our national stature has certainly not gone unnoticed. The brightest minds, the greatest experts, and the most proficient practitioners have analyzed, critiqued, scrutinized, investigated, surveyed, and studied the problem. They have proposed solutions, developed alternatives, launched programs, and commissioned consultations.

All to no avail. The demise continues unabated.

A remarkably parallel situation existed almost three thousand years ago in ancient Palestine. Israel, too, was a late, great nation. Its capital, Jerusalem, had been a sparkling gem among the cities of man. It was powerful, prestigious, and prosperous.

But its fall was consummate. Laid waste by invading armies, looted by wandering marauders, and depreciated by the ravages of time, the city had succumbed to disgraceful ruin.

The walls of the once great capital — symbols of its strength — were shamefully reduced to rubble. Its gates — symbols of its security — were ominously reduced to ash.

The citizens were frustrated, demoralized, and despondent. They had run out of options. They were resigned to their low estate.

But Nehemiah wasn't.

He was a man of vision. A man of strength. A man of character. A man of God. And he was entirely unwilling to sit idly by while the nation lay in ruin.

And so he began the arduous task of restoration. And he began that task by rebuilding the walls.

Those walls would be the foundation of hope and the foundation of security. Nehemiah knew that, if the nation's stature were to be restored in any measure, those walls were the key.

Ultimately, he succeeded. The walls were rebuilt. The greatness was restored. The nation was revived.

If the situation in our own nation is to be turned around, then Christians today are going to have to undertake the same kind of rebuilding, restoring process.

That is what this book is all about.

It explores all the whos, whats, whens, wheres, hows, and whys of rebuilding the "walls" of our nation. It explores the practical details of how Christians can actually help to restore America's greatness. It shows how ordinary churches, ordinary families, and ordinary individuals can accomplish Nehemiah-like feats.

The job won't be easy. It may take quite some time. It most certainly will require tremendous sacrifice.

But it *can* be done.

The walls *can* be rebuilt.

America's greatness *can* be restored.

# PART ONE

## THE CRISIS

It was the best of times, it was the worst of times, it was the age of wisdom, it was the age of foolishness, it was the epoch of belief, it was the epoch of incredibility, it was the season of Light, it was the season of Darkness, it was the spring of hope, it was the winter of despair, we had everything before us, we had nothing before us.

Charles Dickens

# THE HUMANISTIC JUGGERNAUT

He had risen to dizzying heights.

But now, he was plunging to the deepest depths.

Wayne Valis had mingled with the minions of power. As a special assistant to the President, he had been at home in the inner sanctum, knowing the inner workings and the inner secrets. He had walked the hallowed corridors of privilege and prominence. And he had used that privilege and prominence to attain to high station.

But now, as he sat facing the whirring, clicking, flashing cameras of Washington's press corps, he cringed at the thought of his once cherished glories.

"I've come to believe" he began, "especially after my time with Reagan, that there is no ultimate solution to human problems."

His resignation flew in the face of all reason. His despair contradicted the common sense pragmatism that had thrust him to the pinnacle. But his disillusionment would no longer afford him that luxury. His deep and abiding cynicism, grown and nurtured on Capitol Hill, would no longer allow him to continue.

He concluded his press statement in a fluster of frustration. "Every solution that you find contains the seeds of other human problems." The best that the power brokers in Washington could hope to do, he said, would be to "trade *more* vexing problems for *less* vexing problems."

Wayne Valis had become a confirmed and convinced doom-sayer. He had joined the swelling ranks of the hopeless. He had come to realize that even the very best that Washington had to offer was not sufficient unto the day.

5

He was no longer looking for answers. He was resigned to utter despair.

A pall hung over the press corps. Valis had struck an all too sensitive note.

## A Litany of Failure

Wayne Valis was by no means alone in his despondency. A plague of pessimism is sweeping, not just the Washington Mall, but the entire nation.

And for good reason.

Every crisis-wracked, trouble-packed day is but a harbinger of an even more dismal tomorrow, while every policy proposal is but a portent of an even deeper dilemma down the road.

The inability of modern men to find solutions to our societal, personal, and interpersonal problems has left us buried beneath a veritable avalanche of need. It has turned our television broadcasts and our newsprint forecasts into an unrestrained litany of failure:

**Our economy is in shambles.** With deficits skyrocketing and dollar valuations plunging there is hardly a single sector of the economy that offers a ray of hope. Our balance of trade is precariously skewed, our banking system is dangerously over-extended, and our securities market freneticly unstable. Businesses are folding. Currencies are collapsing. Families are struggling. Industries are declining.

And we're in the midst of a "recovery"!

Not surprisingly, this economic mêlée has wrought a bitter harvest of suffering for the poor and disadvantaged. Despite a massive "war on poverty" that has marshalled billions of dollars, thousands of experts, and hundreds of programs into an unprecedented arsenal of societal activism, poverty is actually increasing. One out of every seven Americans falls below the poverty line. Nearly three-fourths of those are women and their children. And as many as two million of them are actually homeless, living by their wits out on the streets.

The shift from the assembly lines to the bread lines has become one of the most prominent features of our economic landscape.

And the powerful, the would-be-powerful, and the wish-they-were-powerful in Washington don't seem to be able to do anything about it.

They don't have answers.

They have failed.

**Our foreign policy is in total disarray.** If things look bad out on the domestic front, they're worse when we look abroad. International tensions have never been higher. Trust within the Western Alliance has never been lower. Stymied from doing right, pressured into doing wrong, our nation's overseas waffling and wavering has caused a global crisis of confidence.

And that's not even the half of it.

Corruption and scandal have stripped the State Department, the CIA, and the Armed Forces of their integrity. Watergate, Korea-gate, Iran-gate, and Contra-gate have emasculated the American international profile, rendering us impotent against Communist imperialism and Third World terrorism.

Again, the experts can offer little in the way of alternatives.

They don't have answers.

They have failed.

**Our criminal justice system is a disgrace.** Overloaded dockets, over-extended budgets, and over-crowded prisons have strained our courts to the limit. Yet at the same time a relativist legal code, an activist judiciary, and an existentialist bar have rendered the system impotent and irrelevant.

So while the incidence of murder, rape, extortion, burglary, narcotics abuse, assault, and vice violations continues to rise, the incidence of justice continues to decline.

Virtually every law and order initiative has fallen short of the mark. Virtually every prison reform proposal has somehow gone astray. Criminals are free on the streets while our law enforcement agencies are handcuffed to unreasonable, unfeasible, ideological mandates.

The experts have commissioned studies, convened discussions, brought in consultants, and poured hundreds of millions of dollars and man hours into bureaucracy's black hole, but the problems remain. The experts have exhausted their repertoire, all to no avail.

They don't have answers.

They have failed.

**Our educational system is a disaster.** Johnny can't read and Susie can't spell. Willie can't write and Alice can't add. Teacher competency is down. Administrative effectiveness is down. Student advancement is down. Test scores are down. Everything, in fact, to do with our public school system is down . . . everything, that is, except crime, drug abuse, illicit sex, and the cost to taxpayers.

As many as twenty-three million Americans are functionally illiterate. Another forty million must be classified as alliterate. And almost all are products of our public school system.

Pilot projects, test programs, experimental curricula, and esoteric methodologies have all been tried and been found wanting. The experts have run out of rabbits to pull from their hats.

They don't have answers.

They have failed. And their failure has not been limited to the areas of economics, foreign affairs, justice, and education. Theirs is a never ending litany of failure. They have failed in community regulation, in environmental protection, in social service provision, in data communication, in technological transformation, and in values transmission.

They have failed.

## A Litany of Horror

Tragically, the faults and foibles of modern men have scarred our social structure more deeply, more grotesquely than mere incompetence could ever have. The refrain of our day is more significant than a dogged rehearsing of a litany of failure. Our whole society seems to be coming apart at the seams. The very unraveling has become a litany of horror:

**Widespread acceptance of abortion has set in motion a domino effect.** Since 1973 nearly twenty-one million children have been ruthlessly slaughtered in our land. Almost four thousand children every day are mutilated and butchered in a holocaust that Hitler could never have hoped to match. In the sterile environs of our hospitals and clinics a wrath of madness is poured out upon the innocents without remorse.

It is in fact that lack of remorse, that dulling of conscience, that is so frightening about the whole abortion mentality. Once a physician brutally subdues his ethical qualms, once he has tasted the blood of his victims, what is to keep him from pursuing his hideous and insidious lust for violence in an ever more barbaric fashion? Absolutely nothing. Which is why infanticide, euthanasia, genetic screening, eugenics, and other "gentle genocides" have crept into common medical practice.

Laboring for a human utopia, the experts have birthed instead an inhuman dystopia.

They have failed.

But not only have they failed, they have unleashed horrors as well.

**The proliferation of pornography has blighted the land.** Filth pours forth in torrents. It is a billion dollar a year industry. Soft porn, hard porn, video porn, kiddie porn, phone porn, cable porn, live porn, snuff porn, gay porn, art porn, music porn, and club porn abound in every community.

Twisting our sensibilities, smothering our discretion, and crushing our inhibitions, it too sets in motion a domino effect. By banishing restraint and moral uprightness to an urban outback, pornography creates an ecology where teen promiscuity, sexually transmitted diseases, unnatural affections, child abuse, homosexuality, sado-masochism, infidelity, divorce, prostitution, unplanned pregnancy, AIDS, and bestiality become inevitable.

In the name of "free speech" and "free expression," the experts have opened a Pandora's Box. Instead of setting us free, the porno plague has placed us in bondage.

Again, the experts have failed. But not only have they failed, they have unleashed horrors as well.

**The "traditional" family is all but extinct.** According to the Census Bureau, the traditional household, one in which the father serves as breadwinner, the mother serves as homemaker, and the children serve as trainees, now accounts for only four percent of all U.S. households. In 1950, this kind of family situation accounted for over eighty percent of all American households.

By contrast, the number of single-parent families has grown sixty percent from 1973 to 1985. Less than a generation ago, in 1950, this kind of family situation accounted for less than eight percent of all the households in the land.

We are no longer witnessing a revolution in the arena of the family. The revolution has already come and gone. No-fault divorce laws, sexual license, the moral assault of abortion and pornography, economic pressure, judicial interference, and educational maladjustment have all combined to cripple the family, threatening its very survival.

Helpless in the face of impending calamity, social analysts, family counselors, and government officials do not know what to do.

Again, the experts have failed.

But not only have they failed, they have unleashed horrors as well.

**Drug use and abuse has grown to crisis proportions**. As if to escape the failures and horrors of modern society, men, women, teens, and even children are resorting to cocaine, PCP, crack, amphetamines, marijuana, heroine, thorazine, lithium, and quaaludes. The drugs offer them a seemingly safe haven from the storms of life. The drugs offer them a respite, however brief, from the tragic realities that bombard them on every side. The drugs offer them an antidote to the bitter wine of modern living.

The dangers do not deter them. The widely publicized deaths of artists, entertainers, and athletes do not frighten them. The ecstasy of release poses too strong an attraction.

Educational programs, media campaigns, rehabilitation projects, and judicial initiatives—the best that the experts can offer—have not even put a dent in America's mad dash for artificial solace.

Again, the experts have failed.

But not only have they failed, they have unleashed horrors as well.

Real horrors.

Unending horrors: cybernetics, algeny, artificial intelligence, surrogate embryonosis, daeliaforcation, wetware implants, hardwiring, cryogenics, viral programming, and dozens of other movements, technologies, and trends that threaten the stability of life, the universe, and everything.

With the disharmonious refrain of modern man's litany of failure and his nefarious litany of horror haunting our every waking moment, is it any wonder that the doomsayers have gained the day? Is it any wonder that men like Wayne Valis simply throw up their hands in despair?

## Humanism

The doctors, lawyers, politicians, social scientists, educators, psychologists, bureaucrats, and various and sundry other experts who have plied their disciplines against the raging problems of our day certainly cannot be faulted for their concern over man's future. Where they went wrong was in taking matters into their own hands. The reason they have failed, the reason they unleashed horrors, is that they completely ignored, and as a consequence violated, God's solutions. Instead of adhering to the wise and inerrant counsel of Scripture, they "did what was right in their own eyes" (Judges 21:25). For all their good intentions, their programs were blatantly man centered.

In other words, they were humanistic.

Humanism is, according to Francis Schaeffer, "the placing of man at the center of all things and making him the measure of all things." Or, as Aleksandr Solzhenitsyn has said, it is "the proclaimed and practiced autonomy of man from any higher force above him." According to humanistic thought, there is no notion of absolute right or wrong. There are no clear-cut standards. Standards flit and flex with the whims of fashion. According to humanistic thought, men's passions are not to be restrained. Instead, passions are to be unshackled, floating free in the ever shifting, ever changing currents of the day.

Western civilization was once informed almost exclusively by the basic tenants of the Christian faith as delineated in the Bible. Scripture was the authoritative voice and conscience of the culture, establishing certain and secure standards, ensuring life, liberty, and justice for all.

But in recent years our culture has witnessed a coup d'état, a dramatic revolution. Christianity has been overthrown and replaced by the totally contrary world and life view of humanism.

So today, when any problem arises, instead of turning to the Bible for answers, our leaders—the experts who determine the course of the future—look to man's own ingenuity. They look, in fact, anywhere and everywhere except to the Bible.

The problem is that such humanistic reasoning is entirely out of synch with reality.

Thus, the litany of failure.

And the litany of horror.

"All Scripture is given by inspiration of God, and is profitable for doctrine, for reproof, for correction, for instruction in righteousness, that the man of God may be complete, thoroughly equipped for every good work" (2 Timothy 3:16-17). Thus, to attempt to solve the perilous problems of modern society without hearing and heeding the clear instructions of the Bible is utter foolishness (Romans 1:18-23). It is an invitation to inadequacy, incompetency, irrelevancy, and impotency (Deuteronomy 28:15). All such attempts are doomed to frustration and failure, as the horrific litanies of modern life have so amply and aptly proven. Humanism and its various programs, policies, and agendas can't work because humanism ignores the fabric of reality (Ephesians 5:6). It is fraught with fantasy (Colossians 2:8).

Only the Bible can tell us of things as they really are (Psalms 19:7-11). Only the Bible faces reality squarely, practically, completely, and honestly (Deuteronomy 30:11-14). Thus, only the Bible can provide genuine solutions to the problems that plague mankind (Psalms 119:105).

## Judgment

There is a direct cause and effect principle at work in our culture, and, in fact, in all cultures. There always has been and there always will be. We reap what we sow (Galatians 6:7).

When a civilization takes seriously the commands of God for every area of life, it most certainly will be blessed. When its laws are in conformity with the Scriptural standards, when its institutions emulate the Scriptural models, and when its character is shaped by the Scriptural edicts, then it will prosper and flourish (Deuteronomy 28:1-14).

If, on the other hand, a civilization ignores the commands of God for every area of life, it will most certainly be cursed. When its laws are in disharmony with Scriptural standards, when its institutions contradict Scriptural models, and when its character defies the Scriptural edicts, then it will flounder and fail (Deuteronomy 28:15-68).

Christianity gives light and life to a land.

Humanism can only offer failure and horror.

The principle is inescapable:

If we sow seeds of obedience to God's Word, we will reap a bounteous harvest of blessing.

But, if we sow seeds of rebellion against God's Word, we will reap a destitute harvest of destruction.

If we sow Christian principles, our culture will reap productivity, stability, and justice. Our problems will be solved. Slowly perhaps, but surely.

On the other hand, if we sow humanistic principles, our culture will reap perversity, despair, and judgment. Our problems will only be magnified. Slowly perhaps, but surely.

This is not a matter of opinion. It is not open to interpretation. The pages of history are literally littered with indisputable evidence.

Godliness brings advance.

Ungodliness brings decline.

No brag, just fact (Deuteronomy 28:1-68).

The Bible tells us that there are at least five progressive stages of judgment in a humanistic nation. Each stage serves as a warning to the people to return to the sanity of righteous obedience to God's Word.

**First, there will be an increase in natural catastrophes** (Isaiah 1:5-9). Whenever judgment befalls a nation, dramatic shifts in weather patterns, geological stability, agricultural productivity, public health and hygiene, and other "natural" phenomena inevitably occur. Rebellious nations invite plagues, famines, earthquakes, volcanic eruptions, catastrophic storms, epidemics, drought, floods, typhoons, and tornadoes. Humanistic nations are thus constantly forced to deal with such things as killer bees, farm crises, AIDS plagues, and San Andreas faults.

Righteous nations, on the other hand, rebuff such judgment. A nation reaps what it sows.

**Second, water will be added to the wine** (Isaiah 1:22). Whenever judgment befalls a nation, a noticeable decline in the quality of products inevitably occurs. Rebellious nations occasion shoddy workmanship, sloppy craftsmanship, and slovenly construction. They are rife with unprofessionalism, slothfulness, discourtesy, sluggardliness, unserviceability, extortion, profiteering, false advertising, shams, cons, and wanton waste. Humanistic nations are thus constantly forced to deal with such things as trade deficits, declining industry, plummeting market shares, massive recalls, and import quotas.

Righteous nations, on the other hand, rebuff such judgment. A nation reaps what it sows.

**Third, the silver becomes dross** (Isaiah 1:22). Whenever judgment befalls a nation, chronic financial crises inevitably occur. Rebellious nations engage in currency devaluation, inflation, deficit spending, and fiat leveraging. Humanistic nations are thus constantly forced to deal with accelerating bankruptcy rates, runaway cost of living increases, unstable exchange ratios, debased currencies, wage and price controls, exorbitant taxation, and money that is not worth the paper it is printed on.

Righteous nations, on the other hand, rebuff such judgment. A nation reaps what it sows.

**Fourth, there is an exchange in leadership** (Isaiah 3:1-5). Whenever judgment befalls a nation good leaders give way to bad, and bad leaders give way to worse. Rebellious nations are an easy target for conspiracy, collusion, corruption, covetousness, and contamination. They seem to breed demagogic, xenophobic, and messianic opportunists who rise to power and prominence. Humanistic nations are thus constantly forced to deal with government scandals, cover-ups, bribes, evasions, investigations, revelations, and resignations.

Righteous nations, on the other hand, rebuff such judgment. A nation reaps what it sows.

**Fifth, the people are taken captive** (Isaiah 5:13-15). When judgment befalls a nation, and it fails to repent during the course of the first four warning stages, it will finally be dragged off into exile. Rebellious nations are weak and gullible in the face of intoxicating philosophies, exotic delicacies, and titillating ideologies. They are lured away from their citadels of strength by the beguiling angels of alien light. Humanistic nations are thus constantly forced to deal with the corrosive incursions of anarchism, totalitarianism, socialism, antinomianism, existentialism, nihilism, and hedonism.

Righteous nations, on the other hand, rebuff such judgment. A nation reaps what it sows.

It doesn't take an expert in sociology, theology, eschatology, or futurology to see that our nation is now undergoing very real and substantial judgment. All five stages of Biblical judgment are everywhere apparent.

Our constant cultural refrain has been a litany of failure and a litany of horror. We have abandoned the hymn of faith for the raucous ditty of humanism. As a result we have gathered a harvest of sorrow and shame. As a result we have succumbed to judgment.

A nation reaps what it sows.

And we have. In abundance.

Doomsayers like Wayne Valis are not as out of touch with reality as we might, at first glance, presume.

## Conclusion

Our nation is in trouble.

Difficulty and trauma bombard us from every side.

Our economy is in shambles. Our foreign policy is in disarray. Our criminal justice system is a disgrace. And our educational system is a disaster.

It's not as if we haven't tried to address and redress all these plaguing problems. It's just that all our attempts have fallen short.

The history of modern social, political, and cultural policy is a veritable litany of failure.

The legacy we leave to our children does not stop at mere incompetence, however. We have entertained a frightful *danse macabre* that has unleashed a litany of horror and a reign of terror on the land.

Widespread acceptance of abortion has set in motion a domino effect of bio-medical madness. The proliferation of pornography, the subversion of the family, the inundation of drug use and abuse, and a hundred other dystopic dilemmas confront us at every turn.

Every proposal and every policy designed to right these wrongs somehow only manages to deepen the downward spiral of destruction.

The reason for this awful situation is that we have abandoned God's answers found in God's Word. Instead of drawing from the deep wellspring of God's wisdom, we have tried to scoop solutions from humanism's shallow slough.

The result has been judgment. We have been judged catastrophically. We have been judged economically. We have been judged juridically. We have been judged ideologically. We have been dragged off into captivity, dominated by the strange and barbaric forces of iniquity.

The humanistic juggernaut has rolled across our land, cutting a wide swath of devastation and despair.

Do not be deceived, God is not mocked; for whatever a man sows, that he will also reap. For he who sows to his flesh will of the flesh reap corruption, but he who sows to the Spirit will of the Spirit reap everlasting life (Galatians 6:7-8).

# THE CONSERVATIVE BETRAYAL

The banners fluttered jubilantly in the blustery breeze along Pennsylvania Avenue. The bands played. The crowds cheered. The camera crews moved into place in anticipation. The moment was electrifying.

As the new President moved into place to take the Oath of Office a tremor of hope shook the entire nation.

Halfway around the globe, the Iranian hostage crisis played out its final drama. America's albatross was no more.

An era had ended.

Another had just begun.

The man who would occupy the Oval Office had the awesome ability to instill confidence, to melt away fear, to nurture optimism, and to inculcate determination. He seemed to be an incarnation of the can-do spirit that had once made our nation the envy of the world. Somehow, he made us believe that the future was not a loathsome responsibility to be resisted at all costs, but a challenging opportunity to be embraced by all means.

And so, Reagan's Revolution began with the highest of expectations and the fondest of dreams.

### The Evangelical Emergence

Chief among the new administration's supporters were evangelical Christians.

And that was a revolution in and of itself.

For almost a full century the entire evangelical community had been in cultural and political hibernation. Thus, despite the largest, most powerful, richest, best organized, and most vocal Christian movement ever, the immoral and unstable humanistic juggernaut was able to gain full control of the cultural apparatus.

For several generations evangelicals had deliberately and self-consciously abandoned the world. They had abandoned the God-ordained mandate to be salt and light (Matthew 5:13-16). They had abandoned the Great Commission to nurture and convert the nations (Matthew 28:19-20). Instead, they had emphasized a view of piety and spirituality based more on the teachings of Plato than on the teaching of Christ.

This kind of religious Platonism — or "pietism" as it is often called — draws a sharp line of distinction between things that are "spiritual" and things that are "material." Believing that the "spiritual" realm is vastly superior to the "physical" realm, pietism tends to spurn all things physical, all things temporal, and all things earthly. Art, music, and ideas are ignored except for their value as propaganda. Activities that do not significantly contribute to inner devotion are neglected. The intellect is held suspect, if not altogether eschewed. And the pleasures of the flesh — regardless of how innocent or sacred — are condemned outright.

According to the thinking of pietism, the Christian's efforts should be exclusively directed toward individualistic, quietistic devotion. Bible study, prayer, Church attendance, and evangelism compose the totality of tasks for the believer. Anything and everything else is a distraction and is worldly.

The Bible asserts that "the earth is the Lord's, and everything in it" (Psalms 24:1). But, according to pietism, only the spirit is the Lord's. All else is tainted beyond reclamation by the awful stench of sin.

The Bible asserts that "Jesus is Lord" over the totality of life (Colossians 1:15-17; Hebrews 1:2-3). According to pietism, Jesus is Lord, but only over a tiny religious cubbyhole in life.

The Bible asserts that Christians are to confront, transform, and lead human culture (Matthew 5:13-16). But, according to pietism, believers are to withdraw from human culture in order to focus on "religious" exercises.

There is no question that the Scriptural mandate includes, as an integral aspect of its plan for victory, deep devotion, piety, and holiness (Matthew 5:48). But it also requires believers to think hard about the nature of Christian civilization (1 Peter 1:13), to develop Biblical alternatives to humanistic programs (Matthew 18:15-20), and to prophesy unhesitatingly to the cultural problems of the age (Isaiah 6:8). These things, too, are true piety.

Pietism's truncated and purblind conception of spirituality simply misses these none too subtle realities.

Thus, by the wholesale adoption of pietism, the Christian community scuttled itself into a cultural backwater. It imprisoned itself behind the walls of an evangelical ghetto. It minimized its impact, sequestered its significance, and stifled its influence.

Humanism's litany of failure and litany of horror went largely unchallenged.

But then came Reagan's Revolution.

The new President awoke the slumbering Church with talk of traditional conservative morality, traditional conservative family life, traditional conservative economics, and traditional conservative values. He roused an evangelical discontent with the rapier conceit of the humanistic juggernaut. He alerted Christians to the dire consequences of their apathy.

Almost overnight a constituency of twenty to thirty million voters re-entered the American electoral process. En masse they joined in an alliance with the traditional conservative "old right" and the traditional conservative "new right", bringing with them an awesome arsenal of money, manpower, and mailing lists.

Thus began an era of hope.

Thus began Reagan's Revolution.

## Mobilizing the Forces

Encouraged by the new President's rhetoric, riled by the isolated harassment of Christian schools, outraged by the selective IRS encroachment, scandalized by blithe discrimination in the schools, alienated by naked intolerance in the media, shocked by the unabashed immorality of popular entertainment, horrified by the unconscionable brutality of abortion, and polarized by the sweeping extremism of the ACLU, the NEA, the NOW, and the PAW, the massive evangelical constituency entered the socio-political fray with an unquenchable eagerness. But while they were ready and willing to tackle the humanistic juggernaut, they were far from able.

Politically naive, socially unsophisticated, theologically uncertain, and culturally immature from generations of retreat and inactivity, Christians were ill-prepared to face the sophisticated, well connected, and supremely qualified establishment. They didn't know what to do, when, where, or how. They didn't know what it took to open doors, pull strings, or scratch backs. They didn't know the ins and outs, the ups and downs, or the whys and wherefores. They didn't know how to play the game and they didn't know the tricks of the trade.

So, they turned to their new comrades-in-arms—the traditional conservatives in the "old right" and the traditional conservatives in the "new right"—for counsel and direction. "Tell us what to do," the Christians cried out. "Put us to work," they exclaimed.

The traditional conservatives were thrilled to say the least. After all, the evangelicals' money, manpower, and mailing lists were nothing to sneeze at.

In exchange, the traditional conservatives tossed the evangelicals a few sops on the party platform: a pro-life plank, a pro-family plank, and a pro-prayer plank.

Reagan's Revolution was off and running.

Or was it?

### Christless Conservatism

What most of the evangelicals failed to realize in their frenzied rush to join the electorate is that Christless conservatism is no better than Christless liberalism. They failed to recognize that conservative humanism is just as dangerous as liberal humanism.

Both brands of humanism are man centered. Both brands of humanism advocate the autonomy of man, the self-sufficiency of man, and the ingenuity of man. And both brands of humanism perpetuate the litany of failure and the litany of horror.

This has been demonstrated all too clearly in the record of Reagan's Revolution:

**Our economy is still in shambles**. Things are, in fact, worse now than they were before. The deficits are higher. The balance of trade is lower. The dollar is weaker. The federal budget is greater. Fiat spending is increasing. Business starts are declining. For the first time, America is no longer a lender nation, but a debtor nation. And the bottom third of this languid and languishing economy—the domain of the poorest of the poor—is in worse shape than at any time since the Great Depression.

For humanism, it's business as usual.

Traditional conservatism has led evangelicals astray.

**Our foreign policy is still in total disarray.** Things are, in fact, worse now than they were before. Our Central American presence has been compromised by scandal. Our Middle Eastern presence has been compromised by indecision. Our European presence has been compromised by recalcitrance. Our South African presence has been compromised by superficiality. Our anti-communist presence has been compromised by opportunism. Foreign affairs have never been more schizophrenic, unstable, or untenable.

It's business as usual.

Traditional conservatism has led evangelicals astray.

**Our criminal justice system is still a disgrace.** The courts are still twisting and manipulating the law. The judges are still pursuing a radical agenda of judicial activism. The Constitution continues to be subverted, converted, and perverted according to the whims and fancies of fashion. Appointments to the federal bench continue according to convention and not conviction.

It's business as usual.

Traditional conservatism has led evangelicals astray.

**Our educational system is still a disaster.** The President's own commission reported that due to public school incompetence we were "A Nation at Risk." We still are. Planned Parenthood still teaches their insidious brand of sex education in the schools. The ACLU still pursues their radical program of curriculum transformation and religious persecution. The NEA still rapes our children's minds with their situational ethics agenda and their values clarification program. The assault on our young is proceeding apace.

It's business as usual.

Traditional conservatism has led evangelicals astray.

**Abortion continues unabated.** An Executive Order could

have halted the treachery long ago. Instead though, more children have been slaughtered during Reagan's Revolution than at any other time in history. New drugs have been introduced. New technologies have been tested. And new methodologies have been accepted. And all at a greatly accelerated rate. Despite all the Abe Lincoln rhetoric, there has been no Abe Lincoln action.

It's business as usual.

Traditional conservatism has led evangelicals astray.

**Pornography continues to proliferate**. Despite the widely publicized Attorney General's Commission, no steps have been taken to curb the flood of perversion in our land. No laws have been passed. No restraints have been instituted. No regulations have been enforced. No sanctions have been filed. Even with the AIDS scare ravaging the land, the government's approach to morality remains rooted in the tired old dogmas of humanism.

It's business as usual.

Traditional conservatism has led evangelicals astray.

**The family is still under assault**. There has been no let up. Reagan's Revolution has yet to call off school board harassment of homeschoolers. It has yet to adjust family welfare disincentives. It has yet to reform no-fault divorce laws. It has yet to advance balanced parental rights or parental protection legislation.

It's business as usual.

Traditional conservatism has led evangelicals astray.

**Drug use and abuse continues to rise**. Again, we've had lots of talk, lots of rhetoric, and lots of concern. But none of that babble has yet to be translated into tangible action. The drugs still find their way into our cities, into our streets, and into our lives.

It's business as usual.

Traditional conservatism has led evangelicals astray.

The church has been betrayed.

Many evangelicals began to suspect that they had been betrayed after the mid-term elections in 1986 when the conservative establishment preferred to give up control of the Senate rather than give Christians any real say-so or afford them any real concessions. It was then that evangelicals discovered that they had been used, that they were only wanted for their money, manpower, and mailing lists, that most of their own political action groups were little more than fund-raising fronts, and that their entire movement had been compromised.

The church should have known better.

## Biblical Progressivism

Evangelicals should have known better than to enter into an alliance with traditional conservatives who espouse traditional values. After all, Biblical faith is anything but traditional. It is anything but conservative.

Biblical faith is progressive.

It is humanism that is innately conservative. Even liberal humanism is innately conservative.

Whether left or right, whether radical or traditional, humanism is conservative in nature.

Biblical faith constantly presses for advance. It breaks old wineskins (Luke 5:37-38).

Humanism constantly presses for stabilization. It relies on old broken cisterns (Jeremiah 2:13).

The Biblical agenda involves righteous change, transformation, sanctification, and ultimate victory at all costs.

The humanist agenda involves preservation, conservation, maintaining the status quo, and cutting losses by any means.

Thus, Biblical faith is innately progressive and optimistic while humanism is innately conservative and pessimistic.

The reason for these totally contrary world and life views is quite simple:

The Bible shows fallen man starting with a corrupted earth: thorns and thistles (Genesis 3:18). Through diligent labor, obedience, thrift, and righteousness, man shapes, and tills, and rules over the earth. Under the guidance of the Holy Spirit he takes it from chaos to order. By the power of the Holy Spirit, he takes it from a wilderness into a garden (Isaiah 51:3; 58:10-12; Ezekiel 36:33-36; Romans 8:19-22). The Bible is the story of redemption. It is the story of paradise restored.

Humanism, on the other hand, looks at things quite oppositely. The story of man for the humanist begins east of Eden in pristine beauty. Man is a "noble savage" living in the harmonious "estate of nature." There is no fall. There is no sin. But then comes civilization. For the humanist, civilization is the harbinger of all mankind's woes: pollution, ecological imbalance, environmental pressure, shortages, and chaos. The best man can hope for is to stall the inevitable: utter desolation. The sun is burning out. The atmosphere is disintegrating. The ecosystem is collapsing. If gamma radiation doesn't kill us all, AIDS will. Man holds a very delicate balance. According to the humanist, life on earth is the story of paradise lost.

Thus, while humanists tremble, fret, and fear in the face of the future, Christians should look forward with anticipation, with hope, and with faith. While humanists are forced to fight to maintain, to conserve, to resist the future, Christians should move ahead, challenging the obstacles, utilizing opportunities, and posing solutions.

Christians can't be conservative. It is contrary to the faith.

Conservatism is the domain of the no-answer-no-hope-no-future humanists.

So when evangelicals bought the traditional conservative party line, they bought a bill of goods. A humanistic bill of goods.

They bought and paid for their own betrayal.

They bought and paid for our betrayal.

### Choose Ye This Day

Evangelicals must choose.

Either they will continue to make peace with Christless ideologies, or they will confront them. Either they will attempt to conserve this poor fallen world, or they will attempt to convert it. Either they will endorse traditional values, or they will endorse Biblical values.

They can't have it both ways. "For what fellowship has righteousness with lawlessness? Or what communion has light with darkness? Or what accord has Christ with Belial? Or what part has a believer with an unbeliever?" (2 Corinthians 6:14-15).

If the only contribution Christians can make to the cultural milieu is a mindless, soulless echo of traditional conservatism's tri-cornered-hat vision of America, then perhaps they ought to return to the safe confines of the evangelical ghetto. And perhaps they ought to silence their claim that the Bible has answers to the tough dilemmas of life.

Clearly, a choice must be made.

"As for me and my house, we will serve the Lord" (Joshua 24:15).

## Conclusion

The evangelical-conservative alliance was heralded as a window of opportunity.

But it has turned out to be something else altogether.

It has turned out to be a door to destruction.

Rhetorically, Christians and conservatives seem to have a number of concerns in common: a determination to make government fiscally responsible, a commitment to protecting personal freedoms, a desire for higher moral standards, a distrust of the lumbering bureaucracy, a high view of family life, a devotion to academic integrity, and a trust in the basic soundness of the Constitutional system. Both evangelicals and conservatives say that they want a healthy deregulated economy, a long-term commitment to ethical uprightness and an end to harassment of families, minorities, churches, and private schools.

But because Christless conservatives do not have the theology or the Spiritual power to back up their rhetoric with action, they wind up betraying the very causes they claim to espouse. And they wind up betraying the Christians that were drawn into their circle of influence.

Conservatism talks the talk. But it simply can not walk the walk.

It was during the conservative administration of Richard Nixon that the gold standard was abolished, that wage and price controls were instituted, that relations were normalized with Communist China, and that abortion was legalized.

It was during the conservative administration of Ronald Reagan that trade was normalized with the Soviet dictatorship, that sanctions were imposed on South Africa, that trade barriers were erected against Japan, and that the government's unfunded liability surpassed a trillion dollars.

Traditional conservatism has led evangelicals astray. It has sold them a bill of goods.

If the Church is to fulfill her commission to convert the nations, conforming them to the image of Christ Jesus, then she must immediately cease trying to conserve the nations, conforming them to the image of traditionalism. If the Church is to hear and heed the Word of God, then she must immediately cease taking counsel from conservative humanists and their cohorts.

There can be no ifs, ands, or buts about it. Christians must choose.

Blessed is the man who walks not in the counsel of the ungodly, nor stands in the paths of sinners, nor sits in the seat of the scornful; but his delight is in the Law of the Lord, and in His Law he meditates day and night (Psalms 1:1-2).

# PART TWO

## THE SOLUTION

If I profess with the loudest voice and clearest exposition every portion of the truth of God except precisely that little point which the world and the devil are at the moment attacking, I am not confessing Christ. Where the battle rages, there the loyalty of the soldier is proved and to be steady on all the battle front besides, is mere flight and disgrace if he flinches at that point.

Martin Luther

THREE

# THE UNCHANGING
# STANDARD

The two candidates squared off beneath the scorching studio lights.

Accusations flew back and forth. Statistics were cited. Endorsements were quoted. Platforms were rehearsed. Platitudes were pronounced. Promises were proferred.

Despite all the glitter and glitz, the hyperbole and hype, the choice between the candidates seemed clear enough.

Dave Thompson was a classic liberal Democrat.

Jim Nolte was a classic conservative Republican.

"The complex dilemmas of modern America," argued Thompson, "preclude simplistic notions of right and wrong, of black and white. Many of the issues facing us can only be distinguished as varying shades of gray."

"Right is right and wrong is wrong," retorted Nolte. "By adhering to America's traditional values we can steer clear of my opponent's hazy gray. By adhering to America's traditional values we can get ourselves back on track. We can regain our greatness."

Predictably, Thompson won the support of organized labor, minorities, gays, feminists, and the media establishment.

Just as predictably, Nolte won the support of local businessmen, middle managers, entrepreneurs, and the evangelical community.

The issues were cut and dry.

Or were they?

Close scrutiny revealed that both candidates favored lifting restrictions on pari-mutuel gambling as a means to supplement state revenues. Both candidates opposed new zoning restrictions that would greatly inhibit the growth of pornographic businesses. Both candidates favored State Board of Education measures designed to regulate and restrict homeschooling activities. Both candidates opposed legislation to restrict the rights of women to abort their unborn children. Both candidates favored state funding for public high school birth control clinics in every public high school. Both candidates opposed school prayer provisions currently under consideration. Both candidates favored a strict regulation of broadcasting access in order to limit the amount of "manipulative TV evangelism."

In short, both candidates were operating from the same humanistic presuppositional base. Thompson was a liberal, but he was a liberal humanist. Nolte was a conservative, but he was a conservative humanist.

Both candidates were wolves among the sheep. One was a wolf in sheep's clothing. The other was just a naked wolf. But no matter how you looked at it, both were wolves.

Even so, Nolte won the enthusiastic support of evangelicals.

He won their support because he continually trumpeted the theme of "America's traditional values."

And "traditional values" sound "Christian."

All too often, though, "traditional values" are like the fruit on Eden's forbidden tree: they look good, delightful, and desirable, but are, in fact, quite contrary to God's will and purpose (Genesis 3:6).

Some of America's "traditional values" include racism, materialism, individualism, centralism, antinomianism, Social Darwinism, hedonism, and latitudinarianism. All of which are unbiblical and immoral. All of which are humanistic.

If Christians are going to help restore America's greatness, if they are going to make a difference in their families, their communities, and their culture, then they are going to have to measure their actions and alliances against something other than the ever-shifting, ever-changing, and ever-evolving standard of humanism.

They are going to have to measure their actions and alliances against the inerrant, immutable, unchanging standard of Scripture.

## Usus Universus

The Bible is the Word of God. It is His revelation of wisdom, knowledge, understanding, and truth. It is not simply a splendid collection of inspiring sayings and stories. It is God's message to man. It is God's instruction. It is God's direction. It is God's guideline, His plumb line, and His bottom line.

From Genesis to Revelation the Bible is God's own Word. Nearly five thousand times throughout, the narrative is punctuated with phrases like "thus saith the Lord," "thus the Lord commanded His people," or "thus came the Word of the Almighty."

Evangelicals have been led astray by humanism's false promise of "mom, baseball, and apple pie" traditional values simply because they have failed to hear and heed the Bible. They have become gullible, malleable, and vulnerable simply because they have failed to measure their actions and alliances against this unchanging standard.

> To the law and to the testimony! If they do not speak according to this Word, it is because there is no light in them (Isaiah 8:20).

Jesus constantly reminded His disciples that the Word of God was to be their only rule for life and godliness, for faith and practice, for profession and confession:

> But He answered and said, "It is written, 'Man shall not live by bread alone, but by every Word that proceeds from the mouth of God'" (Matthew 4:4).

> And it is easier for heaven and earth to pass away than for one tittle of the Law to fail (Luke 16:17).

> Whoever therefore breaks one of the least of these Commandments, and teaches men so, shall be called least in the kingdom of heaven; but whoever does and teaches them, he shall be called great in the kingdom of heaven (Matthew 5:19).

Again and again He affirmed the truth that "All Scripture is God breathed" (2 Timothy 3:16), that it is "useful for teaching, rebuking, correcting, and training in righteousness" (2 Timothy 3:17), and that it "cannot be broken" (John 10:35). He made it clear that He did not come to do away with the Word—to abolish or abrogate it. On the contrary, He came to fulfill it—to confirm and uphold it (Matthew 5:17). He reiterated the fact that every one of "His righteous Ordinances is everlasting" (Psalms 119:160) and that "the Word of God shall stand forever" (Isaiah 40:8).

Jesus was showing His disciples that, unlike human lawmakers, God does not change His mind or alter His standards: "My covenant I will not violate, nor will I alter the utterance of my lips" (Psalms 89:34). When the Lord speaks, His Word stands firm forever. His assessments of right and wrong do not change from age to age: "All His precepts are trustworthy. They are established forever and ever, to be performed with faithfulness and uprightness" (Psalms 111:7-9).

But the Bible is not simply authoritative, revelatory, and eternal. It is also intensely practical (Proverbs 3:5-6). It is the frame for the very fabric of reality (Romans 1:16-32).

**The Bible convicts us of sin and leads us to Christ**. This is what the early Church fathers and the Reformers called *usus pedagogus*: the tutorial application of God's Word.

So then faith comes by hearing and hearing by the Word of God (Romans 10:17).

Therefore the law was our tutor to bring us to Christ, that we might be justified by faith (Galatians 3:24).

What shall we say then? Is the law sin? Certainly not! On the contrary, I would not have known sin except through the law. For I would not have known covetousness unless the law had said, "You shall not covet." But sin, taking opportunity by the commandment, produced in me all manner of evil desire. For apart from the law sin was dead. I was alive once without the law, but when the commandment came, sin revived and I died. And the commandment, which was to bring life, I found to bring death. For sin, taking occasion by the commandment, deceived me, and by it killed me. Therefore the law is holy, and the commandment holy and just and good. Has then what is good become death to me? Certainly not! But sin, that it might appear sin, was producing death in me through what is good, so that sin through the commandment might become exceedingly sinful. For we know that the law is spiritual, but I am carnal, sold under sin. For what I am doing, I do not understand. For what I will to do, that I do not practice; but what I hate, that I do. If, then, I do what I will not to do, I agree with the law that it is good. But now, it is no longer I who do it, but sin that dwells in me (Romans 7:7-16).

**The Bible is also a guide for daily living, a means for attaining our promised victory.** This is what the early Church fathers and the Reformers called *usus normativus*: the normative application of God's Word.

As His divine power has given us all things that pertain to life and godliness, through the knowledge of Him who called us by glory and virtue, by which have been given to us exceedingly great and precious promises, that through these you may be partakers of the divine nature, having escaped the corruption that is in the world through lust (2 Peter 1:3-4).

How can a young man cleanse his way? By taking heed according to Your word. With my whole heart I have sought You; Oh, let me not wander from Your commandments! Your word I have hidden in my heart, that I might not sin against You. Blessed are You, O Lord! Teach me your statutes (Psalm 119:9-12).

Only be strong and very courageous, that you may observe to do according to all the law which Moses My servant commanded you; do not turn from it to the right hand or to the left, that you may prosper wherever you go. This Book of the Law shall not depart from your mouth, but you shall meditate in it day and night, that you may observe to do according to all that is written in it. For then you will have good success (Joshua 1:7-8).

**The Bible is a testimony to the nations, calling them into submission.** This is what the early Church fathers and the Reformers called *usus motivatus*: the motivational application of God's Word.

But you who held fast to the Lord your God are alive today, every one of you. Surely I have taught you statutes and judgments, just as the Lord my God commanded me, that you should act according to them in the land which you go to possess (Deuteronomy 4:5-8).

I, the Lord, have called You in righteousness, and will hold Your hand; I will keep You and give You as a covenant to the people, as a light to the Gentiles, to open blind eyes, to bring out prisoners from the prison, those who sit in darkness from the prison house (Isaiah 42:6-7).

Also today the Lord has proclaimed you to be His special people, just as He has promised you, that you should keep all His commandments, and that He will set you high above all nations which He has made, in praise, in name, and in honor, and that you may be a holy people to the Lord your God, just as He has spoken (Deuteronomy 26:18-19).

**The Bible is a revelation of God's universal societal standards**. This is what the early Church fathers and the Reformers called *usus politicus*: the civil application of God's Word.

Now it shall come to pass, if you diligently obey the voice of the Lord your God, to observe carefully all His commandments which I command you today, that the Lord your God will set you high above all nations of the earth. And all these blessings shall come upon you and overtake you, because you obey the voice of the Lord your God: Blessed shall you be in the city, and blessed shall you be in the country. Blessed shall be the fruit of your body, the produce of your ground and the increase of your herds, the increase of your cattle and the offspring of your flocks. Blessed shall be your basket and your kneading bowl. Blessed shall you be when you come in, and blessed shall you be when you go out (Deuteronomy 28:1-6).

Listen now to my voice; I will give you counsel, and God will be with you: Stand before God for the people, so that you may bring the difficulties to God. And you shall teach them the statutes and the laws, and show them the way in which they must walk and the work they must do. Moreover you shall select, from all the people able men, such as fear God, men of Truth, hating covetousness; and place such over them to be rulers of thousands, rulers of hundreds, rulers of fifties, and rulers of tens. And let them judge the people at all times. Then it will be that every great matter they shall bring to you, but every small matter they themselves shall judge. So it will be easier for you, for they will bear the burden with you (Exodus 18:19-22).

Let every soul be subject to the governing authorities. For there is no authority except from God, and the authorities that exist are appointed by God. Therefore whoever resists the authority resists the ordinance of God, and those who resist will bring judgment on themselves. For rulers are not a terror to good works, but to evil. Do you want to be unafraid of the authority? Do what is good, and you will have praise from the same. For he is God's minister to you for good. But if you do evil, be afraid; for he does not bear the sword in vain; for he is God's minister, an avenger to execute wrath on him who practices evil (Romans 13:1-4).

Christian philosopher Cornelius Van Til has said, "The Bible is authoritative on everything of which it speaks. And it speaks of everything." The witness of "usus pedagogus," "usus normativus," "usus motivatus," and "usus politicus," confirms that truism as truth.

Thus, the Bible has "usus universus": universal value, universal function, universal effect, and universal exclusivity.

If Christians would only hear and heed the Bible as "usus universus," then they would be able to avoid the traps set by inhuman humanism. They would be able to steer clear of the false hope of "traditional values." They would be able to discern the insidious homogeny of candidates like Dan Thompson and Jim Nolte. And they would be able to make a real and substantial difference in their families, their communities, and their culture.

## The Christian Heritage

Whenever and wherever believers have seriously applied Scripture as "usus universus," not only has God sparked genuine revival, but He has provoked a magnificent cultural flowering as well.

**In Byzantium (330-1453), believers applied the Word of God to every area of life**. For more than a millennium after the fall of the Western Roman Empire, the Eastern provinces flourished under a vibrant missionary Church and a benevolent

Christian commonwealth. At a time when Europe was plunged into the depths of the Dark Ages, Byzantine Christian scholars were achieving dramatic advances in mathematics, science, medicine, engineering, and architecture. A profusion of enduring art, music, philosophy, and literature was produced. Some of Christendom's greatest theologians emerged from Byzantium's many excellent schools and academies, including Augustine, Athanasius, Basil, Chrysostom, Cyril, Eusebius, Gregory the Great, and Ignatius. And the legal system produced such renowned Christian statesmen as Constantine, Justinian, Heraclius, and Basil II.

According to chroniclers of the age, the character of the culture was remarkably Christian. Although the capital, Constantinople, naturally attracted a motley collection of political opportunists, imperial aspirants, and rogue tradesmen, successive waves of revival swept through the entire culture, cleansing, converting, and Christianizing every institution from the family to the mercantile associations, from the government to the trade guilds, from the Church to the military. It was, by all accounts, a remarkably pure, upright, moral, stable, Church-going, law-abiding, and Christ-honoring civilization.

Utilizing the Bible as "usus universus," the Byzantine believers made a real and substantial difference in their families, their communities, and their culture. They established true national greatness.

**In Kievan-Rus (988-1923), believers applied the Word of God to every area of life**. As the heirs of the Byzantine milieu, they extended the reach of the Gospel from high on the Russian steppes to deep in the Finnish woods, from the heart of Slavia to the edge of the Balkans, from the fertile plains of the Ukraine to the lush hills of the Crimea. Theirs was one of the richest and deepest abiding Christian civilizations of all time.

As in Byzantium, the Kievan-Rus culture was a seedbed for an aggressive expansion of human achievement. Great advances were made especially in art, music, architecture, drama, literature, navigation, and mercantilism.

And like Byzantium, the Kievan-Rus culture was marked by a distinct reverence for the things of Christ. Travelers often noted how utterly barren the streets of Kiev became during Sunday morning worship. They testified that the entire citizenry attended Church, not out of compulsion, but because the city's more than one hundred and twenty congregations were aflame with revival.

Nearly a millennium later, when Red Army troops finally conquered the Ukraine in 1923, first Lenin and then Stalin were forced to pour out their wrathful persecution upon the still vibrant Church there. It was only after twenty to thirty million of the faithful had been starved and slaughtered that the Soviet dictators were able to bring the region into subjection. Such was the strength of the Bible-centered Kievan-Rus civilization.

Utilizing the Bible as "usus universus," the Kievan-Rus believers made a real and substantial difference in their families, their communities, and their culture. They established true national greatness.

**In the Massachusetts Bay Colony (1620-1776), believers applied the Word of God to every area of life**. When the Pilgrims arrived off Cape Cod to carve out a new life for themselves in this rugged new world, they had but one thing in mind: to establish a thoroughly Christian civilization. They covenanted together to forge from the frontier a distinct Gospel testimony to all the nations of the earth.

Drawing from the already rich legacy of the Reformers in Geneva and the Puritans in England, they planted and nurtured a cultural apparatus that, within a century, would challenge the supremacy of the world's greatest empires and that, within two centuries, would itself become supreme.

The hard work, obedience, faithfulness, stalwartness, and providence of those early Pilgrims paved the way for all the spectacular advances of modern America. It was this Bible-centered culture that gave us Harvard, Princeton, and Yale. It was this Bible-centered culture that gave us the Mayflower Compact, the Declaration of Independence, and the Constitution. It was this Bible-centered culture that gave us such men as Cotton Mather, Jonathan Edwards, Samuel Adams, George Washington, and John Witherspoon. It was this Bible-centered culture that gave us the Great Awakening, the Great Missionary Thrust, and the Manifest Destiny. It was this Bible-centered culture, more than any other, that gave shape to the modern world.

Utilizing the Bible as "usus universus," the Massachusetts Bay Colony believers made a real and substantial difference in their families, their communities, and their culture. They established true national greatness.

Dozens of other, though perhaps less spectacular, examples of Christian cultural flowerings could easily be cited: the Swiss Cantons (1535-1816), the Dutch Commonwealth (1710-1875), the Boer Republic (1737-1814), the Scottish Commonwealth (1572-1721), the British Commonwealth (1682-1910), etc. Whenever and wherever believers have seriously applied Scripture as "usus universus," not only has God sparked genuine revival, but He has provoked a magnificent advance of civilization as well.

## Conclusion

Every civilization in the long and turbulent history of mankind has been built upon some basic moral standard. Some are built on the sand-standard of traditional values. Others are built on the sand-standard of revolutionary values (such values are nothing more than passe or taboo traditional values). But when the rains of disruption descend, when the floods of corruption come, and the winds of belligerence blow, such civilizations inevitably fall (Matthew 7:26-27). Only those civilizations built on the rock-solid standard of Biblical values can withstand the storms of history (Matthew 7:24-25).

The Bible is the frame of the very fabric of reality. To attempt any work, whether it be the work of building a family, building a church, or building culture, without carefully adhering to its dictates and design is utter insanity (Romans 1:16-32).

The Bible convicts us of sin and leads us to Christ.

The Bible guides us in the various tasks of daily living.

The Bible is a testimony to the nations, calling them into submission.

The Bible is a revelation of God's societal expectations and requirements.

Thus, the Bible has "usus universus": universal value, universal function, universal effect, and universal exclusivity.

If Christians today really want to help restore America's greatness, if they want to make a difference in their families, their communities, and their culture the way that the Byzantine,

Kievan-Rus, and Massachusetts Bay Colony believers did, then they are going to have to hear and heed the Word of God. They are going to have to trust and obey.

> All Scripture is given by inspiration of God, and is profitable for doctrine, for reproof, for correction, for instruction in righteousness, that the man of God may be complete, thoroughly equipped for every good work (2 Timothy 3:16-17).

# FOUR

# WORD AND DEED

Actions speak louder than words.

Kicking up dust on the campaign trail, James Washington was never one to mince words. His caustic and forthright oratory did little to win friends and influence enemies for his congressional race. His gangling bravado infuriated the opposition. His gambolent bluster frightened the undecided. And his grandiloquent bombast worried his own party regulars.

Even so, the Democratic contender held his own quite admirably in the pre-election polls. It seemed that no amount of indiscretion, or incongruity, or inconsistency, or incoherence, or incorrigibility, or incompetence, or inappropriateness, or inanity could corrupt the credibility of his campaign.

That was because actions speak louder than words. And for more than twenty years Washington's actions had secured for him the moral high ground. On that, friend and foe alike had to agree.

While still in school in the sixties, he had been a valiant crusader for civil rights. In the early seventies, he demonstrated able leadership as a community organizer in the distressed inner city. Later he pioneered youth programs, drug rehabilitation programs, health care programs, job initiative programs, urban development programs, minority day care programs, enterprise enlistment programs, voter registration programs, and emergency relief programs. By the early eighties, Washington had become a cherished community landmark, recognized for his selfless devotion to the underprivileged and distressed. He was constantly consulted by mayors and governors. He was forever traveling to the nation's capital to testify before various congressional sub-committees.

Because he had *served*, he had earned the respect accorded

him. Because he had *served*, he had earned the authority accorded him. Because he had *served*, he had earned the moral high ground accorded him.

Despite the fact that his incumbent opponent had a much better grasp of the issues, had far more experience in handling the organs of governance, and was much more articulate and personable, Washington held the upper hand in the campaign.

**Servanthood**

The experience of James Washington confirms one of the most basic principles in the Bible: There is a direct connection between service and authority. It is only as men become the benefactors of the people through servanthood that they are able to become the leaders of the people.

Jesus was a servant. He came to serve, not to be served (Matthew 20:20). And He called His disciples to a similar life of selflessness. He called them to be servants (Matthew 19:30).

Sadly, servanthood is a much neglected, largely forgotten Christian vocation today. Most Christians are obsessed with leading. They want headship. They want prominence. They want dominion, not servitude.

Their obsession with power has been, and continues to be, self-defeating, as men like Washington usurp them with simple service.

Jesus made it plain that if Christians want authority, they must not grasp at the reigns of power and prominence. They must serve. It is only by service that they become fit for leadership. Jesus said, "Whoever wishes to be chief among you, let him be your servant" (Matthew 20:27). The attitude of all aspiring leaders "should be the same as Christ's, who, being in very nature God, did not consider equality with God something to be grasped, but made Himself nothing, taking the very nature of a servant, being made in human likeness. And being found in appearance as a man, He humbled Himself and became obedient to death, even death on a cross. Therefore God exalted Him to the highest place and gave Him the name that is above every name" (Philippians 2:5-9 NIV).

This principle is reiterated throughout the Biblical narrative. The theme of the suffering servant who later triumphs, who serves faithfully and then succeeds, is, in fact, the commonest of Scriptural themes.

**Jacob was a servant.** He served his ruthless uncle Laban under difficult and demeaning circumstances for more than fourteen years. But then, God exalted him to high honor and position. His service earned him authority (Genesis 31:1, 36-42).

**Joseph was a servant.** He served faithfully in Potiphar's house only to be falsely charged and imprisoned. But then God raised him up to become Pharaoh's second-in-command. His service earned him authority (Genesis 39:1,7-20; 41:38-43).

**David was a servant.** He served in the court of King Saul as a musician and a warrior. And though the king ultimately turned on him, David remained steadfast. In the end, that faithful service won him the crown (1 Samuel 16-19; 23; 24:20).

**Daniel was a servant.** He served as an exile in the courts of Nebuchadnezzar and Darius. His faithfulness stirred the envy of the power-seekers and the power-brokers. Their vicious plotting landed him in the lions' den, but he prevailed nonetheless. His service earned him victory (Daniel 6:3-28).

In the same way, Paul and Silas won Philippi from a dark, dank dungeon cell. Jeremiah won Judea cloaked in sackcloth and ashes. And Hosea won Israel from under the rubble of a broken home. They won because service leads to authority.

Each one of these great heroes was a servant. And God honored their service with responsibility and respect, power and privilege, glory and greatness. God honored their service with authority.

It is no accident, then, that those who are commissioned by the King of kings to be "witnesses in Jerusalem, Judea, Samaria, and to the uttermost parts of the earth" (Acts 1:8) and "to make disciples of all nations" (Matthew 28:19), are commissioned as servants. Not as overlords.

The Apostle Paul was a servant (Galatians 1:10). That is all he ever aspired to be (Romans 1:1). Similarly, James (James 1:1), Peter (2 Peter 1:1), Epaphroditus (Colossians 4:12), Timothy (2 Timothy 2:24), Abraham (Psalm 105:42), Moses (Nehemiah 9:14), David (Psalm 89:3), and Daniel (Romans 6:20) were *all* known as servants. They all served, and won for themselves authority.

If Christians are going to rebuild the walls of this culture, if they are going to help to restore America's greatness, they are going to have to learn the lost art of servanthood. They are going to have to comprehend the connection between service and authority.

> What does it profit, my brethren, if someone says he has faith but does not have works? Can faith save him? If a brother or sister is naked and destitute of daily food, and one of you says to them, 'Depart in peace, be warmed and filled,' but you do not give them the things which are needed for the body, what does it profit? Thus also faith by itself, if it does not have works, is dead (James 2:14-17).

Modern men are looking for *proof*. They want *evidence*.

When the great heroes of the faith wedded Word and deed, the people of the day got their proof. They needed no further evidence. They could *see* that the Biblical solutions to societal woes were not simply pie-in-the-sky. They were, instead, cause for hope. Real hope.

True service verifies the claims of Scripture. It tells men that there is indeed a sovereign and gracious God who raises up a faithful people. It tells men that God then blesses those people, and gives them workable solutions to difficult dilemmas.

It is not enough for Christians today merely to *believe* the Bible. It is not enough simply to *assert* an innate trust in Scriptural problem-solving. Christians must validate and authenticate their claims. They must *serve*, backing up Word with deed.

Whenever and wherever Christians have effected righteous change in their society, that change has come on the heels of an explosion of good works. From the time of Paul's missionary journeys to the Genevan Reformation, from Athanasius' Alexandrian outreach to America's Great Awakening, Christian cultural influence has always been accompanied by selfless service. Hospitals were established. Orphanages were founded. Rescue missions were started. Almshouses were built. Soup kitchens were begun. Charitable societies were incorporated. The hungry were fed, the naked clothed, and the homeless sheltered. Word was wedded to deed.

This is as it should be. Even today. Christians are to stand before the world as "a pattern of good deeds" (Titus 2:7). They are "to be ready for every good work" (Titus 3:1).

> For the grace of God that brings salvation has appeared to all men, teaching us that, denying ungodliness and worldly lusts, we should live soberly, righteously, and godly in the present age, looking for the blessed hope and glorious appearing of our great God and Savior Jesus Christ, who gave Himself for us, that He might redeem us from every lawless deed and purify for Himself His own special people, zealous for good works (Titus 2:11-14).

Word and deed.

Sadly, that legacy is a lost legacy.

The fact is, the Welfare State humanists—men like James Washington—have absconded with that legacy and taken it for themselves. They have stolen the moral high ground from the Christian community. Despite the fact that their civil rights measures have been more rhetoric than reality and their "war on poverty" has been more a "war on the poor," they have taken a servanthood pose while Christians have been idle and apathetic. Their pose has won for the humanists cultural authority. They have served as the people's benefactors while the Church has become increasingly obsolescent. So, guess who has won the right to rule and judge?

> The kings of the Gentiles exercise lordship over them, and those who exercise authority over them are called benefactors (Luke 22:25).

If Christians are going to help turn this nation around in any measure, then they will have to recapture their place of authority. But in order to do that, they will have to wrestle from the humanists the mantle of servanthood. *They* will have to become the people's benefactors.

## An Open Opportunity

The unchanging standard of Scripture must be matched with the unwavering commitment of servanthood. Only then can Christians hope to overcome the humanist assaults against life and liberty in this land.

Is this not the fast that I have chosen: to loose the bonds of wickedness, to undo the heavy burdens, to let the oppressed go free, and that you break every yoke? Is it not to share your bread with the hungry, and that you bring to your house the poor who are cast out; when you see the naked, that you cover him, and not hide your own flesh? Then your light shall break forth like the morning, your healing shall spring forth speedily, and your righteousness shall be your rear guard. Then you shall call, and the Lord will answer; you shall cry, and He will say, "Here I am." If you take away the yoke from your midst, the pointing of the finger, and speaking wickedness, if you extend your soul to the hungry and satisfy the afflicted soul, then your light shall dawn in the darkness, and your darkness shall be as the noonday. The Lord will guide you continually and satisfy your soul in drought, and strengthen your bones; you shall be like a watered garden, and like a spring of water, whose waters do not fail. Those from among you shall build the old waste places; you shall raise up the foundations of many generations; and you shall be called the Repairer of the Breach, the Restorer of Streets to Dwell In (Isaiah 58:6-12).

The needs are great. Thus, Christians have an open opportunity. They have the opportunity to demonstrate the "usus universus" of the Bible, its universal value, universal function, universal effect, and universal exclusivity.

**The plight of the poor provides believers with an open opportunity.** In 1950, one-in-twelve Americans (about twenty-one million) lived below the poverty line. In 1979, that figure had risen to one-in-nine (about twenty-six million). Today, one-in-seven (nearly thirty-four million) fall below the line.

More than one-fourth of all American children live in poverty (up from 9.3 percent in 1950 and 14.9 percent in 1970). And for black children under the age of six, the figures are even more dismal: a record 51.2 percent.

Today, 81 percent of elderly women, living alone, live in poverty, all too often in abject poverty, up from 37 percent in 1954.

As many as two million Americans are homeless, living out of the backs of their cars, under bridges, in abandoned warehouses, atop street-side heating grates, or in lice-infested public shelters. Even at the height of the Great Depression, when dust-bowl refugees met with the "grapes of wrath" on America's highways and byways, there have *never* been so many dispossessed wanderers.

The fact is, the Reagan Recovery of the 80's never reached into the cavernous depths of the bottom third of the economy. Shelters are bulging at the seams. And social service agencies are buried under an avalanche of need.

What an opportunity!

If only Christians would undertake the God-ordained task of Biblical charity — serving the needy, helping the helpless, and caring for the hopeless — not only would they be able to transform poverty into productivity, but they would regain the moral high ground as well (Proverbs 11:25, 14:21, 28:27). By *serving* the despised and rejected, they would obtain the cultural authority they need to help restore America's greatness.

**The frightening dilemmas posed by the AIDS plague provide believers with an open opportunity.** People are afraid. And rightly so.

In 1980, AIDS was virtually unknown outside Central Africa. Only about one hundred cases had been reported in the United States. By 1982, there had been about a thousand diagnosed cases in the United States, but panic had yet to set in. By 1984, there were nearly a million confirmed cases and the media had begun to hype the story. By 1987, when the number of cases was doubling every ten months, when as many as 32 percent of those cases had broken out of homosexual enclaves and into the general populace, when reports of airborne or insect borne transmissions began to circulate widely, and when medical experts began admitting that a cure was, at best, many years away, the trauma on the entire fabric of American society was everywhere apparent.

Tossed to and fro on waves of doubt, fear, ignorance, intolerance, hopelessness, anxiousness, fatalism, and lasciviousness, an entire generation of Americans has been shaken from their sure and secure cultural moorings.

What an opportunity!

If only Christians would undertake the God-ordained tasks of reconciliation and healing — tending the sick, rebuking the wicked, and forgiving the repentant — not only would they be able to offer the suffering the Medicine of Hope, but they would regain the moral high ground as well (Matthew 10:8; Luke 10:29-37). By *serving* the afflicted, believers would obtain the cultural authority they need to help restore America's greatness.

**The difficulties faced by working mothers provide believers with an open opportunity.** Over the last decade, per capita family income has increased 7.1 percent. At the same time, however, the consumer price index has inflated a whopping 11.2 percent. Add to that the fact that only 20 percent of all United States jobs pay enough to lift a family of four above the poverty line, and working mothers become a foregone conclusion.

In 1970 only 39 percent of America's mothers had entered the work force. By 1980, 54 percent were working. And by 1985, 61 percent were. Today, nearly 47 percent of all American families have both parents working.

According to the Bureau of Labor Statistics, 43 percent of those working mothers have children under the age of six. This poses an additional burden in and of itself: day care cost. Nearly 20 percent of those working mothers are so overextended financially that they cannot afford day care at all and are forced into latch key arrangements for their youngsters.

The emotional pressure, the physical fatigue, and the spiritual entropy that working mothers face day in and day out can be utterly debilitating. And with no relief in sight. Ever.

What an opportunity!

If only Christians would undertake the God ordained task of Biblical compassion—encouraging the distraught, upholding the distressed, and refreshing the discouraged—not only would they be able to help working mothers, but they would regain the moral high ground as well (Isaiah 1:17; James 1:27). By *serving* the immediate emotional, physical, and spiritual needs of women and their children, believers would obtain the cultural authority they need to help restore America's greatness.

**The isolation and frustration faced by the handicapped provide believers with an open opportunity.** They are the forgotten and the neglected. And there are millions of them.

According to the best statistics available, as many as 16.3 percent of all Americans (or about thirty-seven million) suffer from some sort of crippling disability—congenital or accidental. There are 6.6 million mentally retarded Americans, with an additional 15.4 million suffering from severe learning disorders. There are at least 1.2 million men, women, and children with total hearing loss, and 6.4 million with total visual impairment. Still another 6.6 million are restricted by paralysis, atrophy, deformity, amputation, degeneration, or immobility.

Abandoned by families, shunned by peers, frustrated by dependency, and incapacitated by loneliness and doubt, the handicapped are all too often society's pariah.

What an opportunity!

If only Christians would undertake the God-ordained tasks of nurturing and sheltering—cherishing the uncherished, respecting the unrespected, and loving the unloved—not only would the handicapped be grafted into the productive, contributive main-stream, but believers would regain the moral high ground as well (Psalm 82:4; Acts 20:35; Luke 14:12-14). By *serving* the disabled, believers would obtain the cultural authority they need to help restore America's greatness.

**The awful calamity facing displaced homemakers provides believers with an open opportunity.** The liberalization of divorce laws, the breakdown of family solidarity, and runaway immorality have combined to create a whole new underclass in American society: the abandoned housewife.

The number of displaced homemakers rose 28 percent between 1975 and 1983 to 3.2 million women. Another 20 percent increase from 1983 to 1987 brought that number to nearly four million. An astonishing 61 percent of those women suddenly left alone had children under the age of ten at home.

Often without job skills and stranded without alimony or child support, as many as 70 percent of these women make less than $10,000 a year, and 50 percent are employed at minimum wage or less. It is, thus, readily apparent why a full 75 percent of all Americans living below the poverty line in the United States are women and their children.

Caught between traditionalism and feminism, these women have no advocate. No matter where they turn, they don't fit in. They know no context.

What an opportunity!

If only Christians would undertake the God-ordained task of ministering to "orphans and widows"—upholding the weak, upbraiding the lax, and uplifting the vulnerable—not only would women be given their proper due, but believers would regain the moral high ground as well (Exodus 22:22; Psalm 146:8-9). By *serving* displaced homemakers, believers would obtain the cultural authority they need to help restore America's greatness.

**The severe crisis in education provides believers with an open opportunity.** According to the United States Department of Education, twenty-three million Americans are functionally illiterate. Just fifty years ago, only 1.5 percent of white, native-born Americans struggled with this liability. Today that figure has peaked at more than 10 percent. Urban blacks fifty years ago faced an illiteracy rate of about 9 percent. Today the figure is an astonishing 40 percent. And this despite a multi-billion dollar splurge by the government schools all across the United States.

Even in the area of physical fitness the public schools are a dismal failure. The President's Council on Physical Fitness found that 40 percent of boys aged 6-12 and 70 percent of all the girls could not do more than one pull-up. Nearly 55 percent of the girls could not do any. Half of the girls aged 6-17 and 30 percent of the boys aged 6-12 could not run a mile in less than ten minutes. Almost 45 percent of the boys and 55 percent of the girls could not hold their chin over a raised bar for more than ten seconds. And 40 percent of the boys could not even reach beyond their toes while seated on a floor with legs outstretched.

Apparently, Johnny can't read and Susie can't spell. Willie can't write and Alice can't add. And all four of them are terribly out of shape.

According to another presidential study, the demise of America's schools has made this once great land "a nation at risk."

What an opportunity!

If only Christians would undertake the God-ordained tasks of teaching and training—establishing schools, equipping communities, and preparing for the future—not only would the blight of ignorance be banished, but believers would regain the moral high ground as well (Deuteronomy 6:4-9; Ephesians 6:4). By *serving* the young, believers would obtain the cultural authority they need to help restore America's greatness.

Opportunity after opportunity presents itself through service: to the elderly, to the victims of child abuse, to women in crisis pregnancies, to recovering alcoholics, to the terminally ill, to single parents, to repentant homosexuals, to the mentally ill, and to drug addicts on the rebound.

Walk in wisdom seizing the opportunities and redeeming the time (Colossians 4:5).

Christians must learn to recognize and seize these opportunities. They must begin to comprehend the pivotal and powerful influence that service plays in the flow of human history. They must wed Word and deed.

### The Pattern of the Past

It has been done before.

**Yaroslav the Wise (996-1054) understood full well the connection between service and authority.** Instead of demanding absolute and unquestioned allegiance at the outset of his reign, the young Scandinavian-Varangian monarch wooed the hearts of his people with service, selflessness, and sacrifice.

All along the Mongol steppes Yaroslav built churches, schools, hospitals, and trading centers. He adorned the Eastern Slavic cities within his domain with the signposts of gracious servanthood: orphanages, monasteries, charitable societies, almshouses, and chapels. He carved out of the dense woods that lined the Dnieper River a gem of a civilization, rooted in Christian charity, piety, and productivity. He did not merely *believe* the unchanging standard of Biblical dogma, he *obeyed* the unwavering mandate of Biblical service. He wed Word and deed.

And, as a result, he won the confidence and respect of his society. He won cultural authority.

**Anselmo Adornes (1377-1428) understood full well the connection between service and authority.** The Genoan burgher built a magnificent chapel in the heart of the Flemish city of Brugges to commemorate the bravery of his ancestors, Peter and Jacob Adornes, who were slain during the Crusades. The church, a replica of Jerusalem's Church of the Holy Sepulchre, was to memorialize both their sacrificial courage and the faith that impassioned that courage. That was why Adornes built anter-rooms for the sick, hostels for the traveler, and alms-houses for the poor immediately adjacent to the chapel. He did not want his memorial to be a mausoleum or a museum, but a living testament to service and selflessness.

Adornes did not merely *believe* the unchanging standard of Biblical dogma, he *obeyed* the unwavering mandate of Biblical service. He wed Word and deed.

And, as a result, he won the confidence and respect of his society. He won cultural authority.

**Charles Haddon Spurgeon (1834-1892) understood full well the connection between service and authority.** Known as the Prince of Preachers, the great Victorian pastor set his heart on winning his city. And though his oratory was renowned far and wide for its beauty, clarity, and spiritual efficacy, he did not entrust that great task to mere pulpiteering.

Spurgeon was a servant. During his ministry in London's inner city, he founded and oversaw over sixty different charitable ministries, including hospitals, colporterage societies, orphanages, almshouses, schools, missions, literature crusades, and annuity guilds. He did not merely *believe* the unchanging standard of Biblical dogma, he *obeyed* the unwavering mandate of Biblical service. He wed Word and deed.

And, as a result, he won the confidence and respect of his society. He won cultural authority.

Dozens of other examples of Christian service leading to cultural prominence could easily be cited: Augustine in Hippo (354-430), Bernard of Clairveaux in France (1090-1153), John Wyclif in England (1329-1384), Jan Hus in Bohemia (1374-1415), and Dwight L. Moody in America (1837-1899). From Francis of Assisi to Francis Schaeffer, from Brother Oxam to Mother Theresa, Christians have earned the right to speak prophetically and authoritatively to their culture by serving the needy. And that's a model Christians today had best pay heed to, because it's the only model that works.

## Conclusion

One of the most basic principles in the Bible is that there is an inseparable link between authority and service. Authority cannot simply be asserted. It must be earned.

Historically, the community of believers has understood this principle very well. As a result, they made good works a central priority in their mission to the world. That is why Christians have always had such a disproportionate influence in the societies and cultures they've lived in. Actions speak louder than words.

But all that has changed of late. Christians have abandoned their legacy of service. So at a time when dire poverty, raging plagues, and awful neglect should be driving vast hoards into the arms of the Church, those hoards are running instead to liberal humanists like James Washington.

It is not enough to sound the alarms, alert the forces, proclaim the message, and denounce the enemy. The army of Christ must be mobilized for *service*. Like Yaroslav, Adornes, Spurgeon, and the many other faithful Christians who have gone before, believers today will have to return to the unchanging standard of Scripture *and* to the unwavering standard of servanthood if they wish to have any hope of restoring America's greatness.

> For by grace you have been saved through faith, and that not of yourselves; it is the gift of God, not of works, lest anyone should boast. For we are His workmanship, created in Christ Jesus for good works, which God prepared beforehand that we should walk in them (Ephesians 2:8-10).

# FIVE

# TRUE SPIRITUALITY

When Alexis de Tocqueville visited America over one hundred fifty years ago, he observed that "America is great because America is good."

But today, men are offering an entirely different explanation for America's national stature.

The scene resembled a New Year's Eve celebration, or perhaps a homecoming pep rally. The great hall was filled with bright banners, streamers, balloons, and confetti. A brass band ran through an energetic repertoire of old march tunes and patriotic hymns. Buttons, badges, placards, and hats, festooned with happy slogans and clichés, were buoyed above the crowd by hundreds of grasping, reaching, and shoving hands. Boisterous chants, shouts, songs, and cheers rose up again and again, as one speaker after another enumerated America's blessings and blessedness for the crowd.

It was a convention for the no-longer-silent Silent Majority. It was a rally for the "religious right": a vintage harvest of eager Christian activists sheaved by and for traditional political conservatives.

Each of the podium pounding pulpiteers who took the stage reminded his listeners of America's grand glorious heritage. "America is great because of the masterful Constitution our forefathers endowed us with," they would say. "America is great because of the separation of powers," they would say. "America is great because of checks and balances. America is great because of one man-one vote. America is great because of trial-by-jury, a two-party system, a strong national defense, a comprehensive bill of rights, no taxation without representation, an independent judiciary, strict construction, original intent, states' rights, freedom of speech, law and order, and the right of appeal." They said it with poignancy, patriotism, and passion. And the throng applauded in acclamation.

Unlike de Tocqueville, who believed that America's greatness was a matter of character apart from juridical matters, these men attributed that greatness to external, mechanical, legal, and historical circumstances. They even believed that by skillfully combining incentives and disincentives or by artfully devising the correct environment, that greatness could be preserved: enacting the right bills, electing the right politicians, reclaiming the right legacy, recalling the right precedents, and restoring the right priorities.

## National Greatness

It is true that the Ten Commandments hang over the head of the Chief Justice in the Supreme Court building as a reminder of the origin and root of American Law. It is true that both the House and Senate chambers are adorned with the words "In God We Trust." It is true that the Capitol Rotunda displays the figure of the Crucified Christ and the words "The New Testament according to the Lord and Saviour Jesus Christ." It is true that the Great Seal of the United States is inscribed with the phrase "Annuit Coeptis" (God has smiled on our undertaking). It is true that the Library of Congress is emblazoned with the Psalmist's words "the heavens declare the glory of God, and the firmament showeth His handiwork." It is true that the Washington Monument is capped with the words "Praise be to God." It is true that the Constitution is based upon a Trinitarian model, depends upon the Old Testament Hebrew Republic for its institutional structure, and overtly affirms the primacy of the Sabbath and the sovereignty of God's rule.

All those things are true.

But as true as they may be, they are not, in and of themselves, evidence or assurance of America's greatness — past, present, or future.

National greatness does not spring from an accumulation of archival antiquities or architectural details. It does not spring from documents or precedents. It does not spring from constitutions or legislations.

Instead, it springs from righteousness. It springs from goodness. It springs from character. It springs from true spirituality.

Righteousness exalts a nation, but sin is a reproach to any people (Proverbs 14:34).

A throne is established by righteousness (Proverbs 16:12).

In righteousness you shall be established; you shall be far from oppression (Isaiah 54:14).

The nation of Israel had a remarkable heritage, to say the least. They were the apple of God's eye (Zechariah 2:8). They had carefully institutionalized right worship, right judicial structures, right civil structures, and right economic structures (Isaiah 58:2). According to every conceivable external measure — constitutional and institutional — Israel was a great nation (Isaiah 1:11-15).

Yet, God judged them.

God looked upon the nation and found them sorely lacking. He looked and found their national character riddled with transgression and iniquity. He found wickedness and corruption, *despite* their apparent external adherence to the letter of the Law (Isaiah 1:4-12).

Israel had reduced the faith to a series of formulas. They had emptied it of its spirit and had left only the shell of law. They made the same mistake that the Pharisees and Galatian Christians would later make: believing that certain man-made works, laws, structures, and systems can give rise to national and cultural greatness.

## Magic

The basic difference between Christianity and humanism is that the Biblical faith is *a response to Truth* while the man-centered faith is *an attempt to manipulate God*. The Biblical faith aims at God's satisfaction, while the man-centered faith aims at self-satisfaction.

The Biblical faith is thus concerned with character, content, and substance, while the man-centered faith is concerned only with physical, material, and external appearances.

Throughout the ages, men like Cain have *used* structural religion to get what they want (Genesis 4:3-8; Hebrews 11:4; 1 John 3:12). Men like Balaam have *used* structural religion to control their circumstances (Numbers 31:16; 2 Peter 2:15; Revelation 2:14). Men like Korah have *used* structural religion to enhance their own position (Numbers 16:1-3; 31-35). Cain, Balaam, and Korah all believed in the universal power of legal and structural formulas. They believed that they could manipulate both human society and natural elements with law. They also believed that even God would be forced to conform to the desires and demands of men who acted in terms of law: If men would only say certain things, or do certain things, or believe certain things, or enact certain things, then God would *have to* respond. In a very real sense, they believed that *man* controlled his own destiny, using rituals and formulas like *magic* to save mankind, to shape history, to govern society, and to control God.

That kind of rank humanism has always been condemned in the Bible. Salvation by works, salvation by law, salvation by legislation, salvation by education, salvation by constitution—or however this notion may be conceived—is utterly heretical. It is heretical by Old Testament standards as well as by New Testament standards. It was repudiated by Abraham, Moses, and Isaiah no less vehemently than by Paul, John, and Peter (Romans 4:3; Galatians 3:6; Deuteronomy 27:26; Isaiah 1:10-18; Romans 9:32; John 5:25; 2 Peter 1:3-4).

Structural legalism is heresy, plain and simple. It abolishes the significance of the cross (Galatians 5:11). It makes light of Christ's sacrifice (Galatians 2:21). It nullifies the work of the Holy Spirit (Galatians 3:3-5). It abrogates the necessity of grace (Romans 4:4). "Faith is made void and the promise is unfilled" (Romans 4:14), because it makes man and man's ability the measure of all things (Matthew 15:6-9). Thus, structural legalism is nothing more than humanism in disguise.

It is always the inclination of sinful men to reject God's grace "going the way of Cain, rushing headlong into the error of Balaam, and perishing in the rebellion of Korah" (Jude 11). That is why statism is so predominant among rebellious men and nations. After all, if structural legalism *can* save mankind, shape history, govern society, and control God, then obviously men should work to institute a total Law-Order. If the rituals and formulas of law are indeed like magic, then men must erect a comprehensive state structure to govern men comprehensively. If national greatness can be concocted out of an artful development of laws, constitutions, traditions, systems, structures, and precedents then men must create and exalt, or restore and extol those mechanical devises.

**Communism is a saving Law-Order.** It attempts to rule every aspect of life and to solve every problem in life through the agency of an omnipotent, omnipresent structural state system.

**Modern Liberalism is a saving Law-Order.** It, too, attempts to create a messianic state structure, offering salvation by law. It attempts to create a top down formalized government, manufacturing goodness and grace by legislation. Whenever any problem arises, instead of relying upon Almighty God and His guidance in the Word, advocates of the liberal state rush to the bar with a whole series of new rules, regulations, and laws.

**Traditional Conservatism is also a saving Law-Order.** Like Communism and Modern Liberalism, traditional conservatism focuses on external devices, mechanical systems, and structural solutions to society's problems. Liberals may see salvation in a *new* Constitution where Conservatives see salvation in an *old* Constitution, but it is clear enough, *both are looking to some document* for their ultimate hope. Liberals and Conservatives are, thus, only divided on the incidentals. On the essentials — their humanism — they are united.

The *only* alternative to these insidious and tyrannical Law-Order systems is a Biblical society marked by true spirituality and righteousness. The *only* alternative to the notion that national greatness can be achieved by structural legalism is a national character shaped by Biblical character traits.

Christians must not assume that if only they could pass a few good laws, or elect a few good legislators, or appoint a few good judges, or restore a few good traditions that they will ensure America's recovery.

America's *character* must change, not just her laws. America's *character* must change, not just her judges. America's *character* must change, not just her schools, her media, her legislation, or her priorities. And in order for *America's* character to change, the character of *America's Christians* must change.

Only then will those Christians be able to rebuild the walls of this culture. Only then will they be able to help restore America's greatness. Repentance, revival, and righteousness among God's own precedes greatness. It always has. It always will.

> If My people who are called by My name will humble themselves, and pray and seek My face, and turn from their wicked ways, then I will hear from heaven, and will forgive their sin and heal their land (2 Chronicles 7:14).

National character begins with Christian character. National greatness begins with Christian greatness.

## Biblical Character Traits

In writing to the Corinthian Christians—who were sorely divided over structural and legal questions—the Apostle Paul provided a succinct definition of righteousness. Though not exhaustive, Paul's definition does afford believers with a panoramic perspective of essential Biblical character traits:

> Watch, stand fast in the faith, be brave, be strong. Let all that you do be done with love (1 Corinthians 16:13-14).

If Christians are going to rebuild the walls of this culture, if they are going to help to restore America's greatness, they must begin to exemplify this kind of Christian character. They must model it for the nation. They must reject humanism's myth of legal and structural messiahs and begin to demonstrate alertness, steadfastness, bravery, strength, and tender-heartedness. These are the ingredients of national greatness. These are the ingredients of true spirituality.

**First, Christians must be sober, watchful, and alert if America is to be restored to greatness.** It is not enough simply to *believe* the Bible. It is not enough simply to *serve* the needy. Christians must display a genuinely righteous character. And a cornerstone of that character is *alertness*.

All Christians are called to watch over themselves (Deuteronomy 4:15, 23; Revelation 3:2-3). They are to watch over their relationships (Exodus 34:12), to watch over their hearts (Proverbs 4:23), to watch over their lips (Psalm 141:3), to watch over the paths of their feet (Proverbs 4:26), and to watch over their moral conduct (Revelation 16:15). They are to be alert to the call of Christ (Ephesians 5:14), the judgment of Christ (Micah 7:7), and the coming of Christ (Matthew 24:42-43). They are to be alert in spiritual warfare (Ephesians 6:18) and alert in prayer (Colossians 4:2). They are to be alert to the snares of their enemies so that they fall into no temptation (1 Peter 5:8).

Therefore let us not sleep, as others do, but let us watch and be sober (1 Thessalonians 5:6).

Awake, awake! put on strength, O arm of the Lord! Awake as in the ancient days, in the generations of old. Are you not the arm that cut Rahab apart, and wounded the serpent? (Isaiah 51:9).

Of such character is true spirituality made. Of such character is greatness made.

**Second, Christians must be faithful, steadfast, and unwavering if America is to be restored to greatness**. It is not enough simply to *believe* the Bible. It is not enough simply to *serve* the needy. Christians must display a genuinely righteous character. And a cornerstone of that character is *steadfastness*.

All Christians are called to stand firm in the faith (2 Thessalonians 2:25). They are to be steadfast in the midst of suffering (1 Peter 5:9), in the face of strange teaching (Hebrews 13:9), and in times of trying circumstances (James 1:12). They are to be steadfast in good-works (Galatians 6:9), in enduring love (Hosea 6:4), in conduct (Philippians 1:27), in decision-making (1 Kings 18:21), and in absolute loyalty to the Lord (Proverbs 24:21).

Therefore, my beloved brethren, be steadfast, immovable, always abounding in the work of the Lord, knowing that your labor is not in vain in the Lord (1 Corinthians 15:58).

Yet the righteous will hold to his way, and he who has clean hands will be stronger and stronger (Job 17:9).

Of such character is true spirituality made. Of such character is greatness made.

**Third, Christians must be valiant, courageous, and brave if America is to be restored to greatness**. It is not enough simply to *believe* the Bible. It is not enough simply to *serve* the needy. Christians must display a genuinely righteous character. And a cornerstone of that character is *bravery.*

All Christians are called to be fearless in the Lord (Isaiah 12:2). They can face down adversity with great courage because of God's omnipotence (2 Chronicles 32:7), because of His omniscience (Psalm 139:13-19), and because of His omnipresence (Psalm 118:6). They are to be brave in the face of their enemies (Deuteronomy 31:6), and brave in the midst of chastisement (Job 5:17-24). They are to show valor in obedience to the Word of God (Joshua 23:6), for the sake of His people (2 Samuel 10:12), and in all their service (1 Chronicles 28:20).

> For God has not given us a spirit of fear, but of power and of love and of a sound mind (2 Timothy 1:7).

> The wicked flee when no one pursues, but the righteous are bold as a lion (Proverbs 28:1).

Of such character is true spirituality made. Of such character is greatness made.

**Fourth, Christians must be mighty, stalwart, dynamic, and strong if America is to be restored to greatness.** It is not enough simply to *believe* the Bible. It is not enough simply to *serve* the needy. Christians must display a genuinely righteous character. And a cornerstone of that character is *strength.*

All Christians are called to be strong in Christ (2 Corinthians 10:3-6). God has not given them a spirit of weakness but of power (2 Timothy 1:7). The Gospel comes in power (1 Thessalonians 1:5). The Kingdom comes in power (1 Corinthians 4:19), and salvation comes in power (Romans 1:16). This is a power that the wicked can never know (Matthew 22:29), but every believer is already anointed with it (Luke 24:49). They have been endowed with the strength to witness (Acts 1:8), to labor (Colossians 1:29), and to do every good thing (Philippians 4:13). Christ has given Christians the strength of His might (Ephesians 1:9), and the strength of His grace (2 Timothy 2:1).

> He gives power to the weak, and to those who have no might He increases strength. Even the youths shall faint and be

weary, and the young men shall utterly fall, but those who wait on the Lord shall renew their strength; they shall mount up with wings like eagles, they shall run and not be weary, they shall walk and not faint (Isaiah 40:29-31).

Of such character is true spirituality made. Of such character is greatness made.

**Finally, Christians must be respectful, affectionate, and tenderhearted if America is to be restored to greatness.** It is not enough simply to *believe* the Bible. It is not enough simply to *serve* the needy. Christians must display a genuinely righteous character. And a cornerstone of that character is *tenderheartedness*.

All Christians are called to be longsuffering in love and tenderness. They are to show love to strangers (Deuteronomy 10:19) as well as neighbors (Leviticus 19:18), to enemies (Matthew 5:44) as well as brethren (1 Peter 3:8). In all things, at all times, they are to be examples of love (1 Timothy 4:12), abounding in love (Philippians 1:9), and walking in love (Ephesians 5:2). They are to comfort one another in love (Colossians 2:2), greet one another in love (Titus 3:5), provoke one another in love (Hebrews 10:24), and labor with one another in love (1 Thessalonians 1:3). For love is the royal law (James 2:8).

> Though I speak with the tongues of men and of angels, but have not love, I have become as sounding brass or a clanging cymbal. And though I have the gift of prophecy, and understand all mysteries and all knowledge, and though I have all faith, so that I could remove mountains, but have not love, I am nothing. And though I bestow all my goods to feed the poor, and though I give my body to be burned, but have not love, it profits me nothing (1 Corinthians 13:1-3).

Of such character is true spirituality made. Of such character is greatness made.

### Historical Precedents

Whenever a nation has emerged from the vast sea of international mediocrity to demonstrate true greatness, invariably the Christians of that nation have modeled true spirituality. Taking the cultural lead position they willfully wove Godly character into the national fabric.

**When Gerald of Ridfort chronicled his visit to the Kingdom of Jerusalem in 1175, he emphasized the contribution that Christian character had made in the development of that nation's greatness.** The small fiefdom of crusaders and pilgrims was noted throughout Christendom as a paragon of virtue and greatness. Despite the fact that the young king Baldwin IV was continually assailed by the rowdy escapades of European mercenaries, unscrupulous adventurers, and Ayoubid terrorists, he ruled over a people and a culture that flourished and prospered. According to the Flemish Knight Gerard, the challenges only served to call out the best in the nation. They served to call out alertness, steadfastness, bravery, strength, and tenderheartedness. They served to call out true spirituality.

**When Philaret Romanov chronicled his visit to the Republic of Geneva in 1563, he emphasized the contribution that Christian character had made in the development of that nation's greatness.** The small Swiss canton was at the height of its Reform. Calvin was still preaching and teaching. Commerce was brisk and prosperous. Culture was lively and provocative. And piety was universal and infectious. According to the Russian monk Philaret, the Reformation had served to transform the quaint community nestled in the Lac Lehman Valley into an international symbol of greatness. It had served to invoke alertness, steadfastness, bravery, strength, and tenderheartedness from the harsh realities of pioneer settlements. It had served to provoke true spirituality.

**When Alexis de Tocqueville chronicled his visit to the United States in 1834, he emphasized the contribution that Christian character had made in the development of this nation's greatness.** The rapidly expanding American "experiment" was the marvel and fascination of the entire Western world. Industry was flourishing. Cities were growing. Farms were prospering. And the arts were proliferating. According to the French noble de Tocqueville, the Christian faith—setting pulpits aflame and communities apace—had given rise to their vibrant democracy. It had harvested alertness, steadfastness, bravery, strength, and tenderheartedness from the harsh realities of pioneer settlements. It had served to provoke true spirituality.

A medieval fiefdom, a renaissance republic, and a modern

democracy—each with very different laws, constitutions, traditions, systems, and structures—achieved greatness. They achieved greatness because they manifested Biblical character traits. And they manifested Biblical character traits because Christians took the cultural lead and modeled true spirituality.

## Conclusion

Modern America is the special beneficiary of a marvelous heritage. But neither the traditions of freedom, the legal structure, nor the Constitutional framework have in and of themselves the makings of greatness. National greatness *produces* such things, it is not derived from them. Instead, national greatness is a function of character.

When a nation becomes righteous, she becomes great. When a nation begins to display Biblical character traits she begins to achieve greatness. But *only* then.

If Christians are going to rebuild the walls of this culture, if they are going to restore America's greatness, they are going to have to inculcate alertness, steadfastness, bravery, strength, and tenderheartedness, first in their own lives, and then in society at large. They are going to have to model true spirituality.

It is not enough simply to believe the Bible and serve the needy. Genuine Christian character must shine forth as a beacon in the night, leading the culture to Christ. Leading the culture to greatness.

> You are the light of the world. A city that is set on a hill cannot be hidden. Nor do they light a lamp and put it under a basket, but on a lamp stand, and it gives light to all who are in the house. Let your light so shine before men, that they may see your good works and glorify your Father in heaven (Matthew 5:14-16).

SIX

# UNDAUNTED VISION

He stood on the courthouse steps, stern faced but confident. "Look, I've seen this kind of thing happen any number of times before," he said, turning to a gaggle of local reporters. "These folks get all riled up about this issue or that, and start to bully their way into the precinct process. But then the harsh political realities begin to set in and before you know it, they're gone." He paused, gave the cameras a look of calm experience, and then swept his arm dramatically across the sky, "They're like the Swallows of Capistrano—here but for a season." And with that bit of theatrical ease, he turned on his heel and left.

A practiced politician, Harlan Payne knew just how to play circumstances to his best advantage. Even difficult circumstances.

He had just been ousted from his precinct chair, a post he had held for more than fifteen years. During that time he had served his city as *the* Republican Party power-broker and king-maker. He had survived takeover threats by libertarian fringe groups and Birchers, by movement conservatives and LaRouchies, by neo-federalists, and Moonies. But, in a single indelicate move, he was forced out by a coalition of political neophytes from the Religious Right.

Payne wasn't worried though. He knew that Christian activism was probably nothing more than a passing fancy—the latest pop-evangelical fad. As soon as the newness wore off, he'd be back in power and party matters would settle into the normal routine.

Sure enough. He was right. Less than eighteen months later the power-broker and king-maker was once again pulling the strings and setting the stage for the political establishment.

The Swallows of Capistrano had indeed been there "but for a season."

## Future Orientation

Successful cultural action is a multi-generational affair. It demands *commitment* over the long haul: a commitment to the unchanging standard of servanthood, and a commitment to true spirituality.

That kind of commitment is what the Bible calls *vision*. It is the willingness to labor unceasingly for the cause of the truth. It is the willingness to sacrifice unselfishly for the sake of the faith. It is the willingness to bypass immediate gratification, instant satisfaction, and momentary recognition for the good of the future. Where *faith* is "the assurance of things hoped for" (Hebrews 11:1), *vision* is "the hope of things assured of." Where *faith* is "the conviction of things not seen" (Hebrews 11:1), *vision* is "the seeing of those convictions."

Visionary men are confident, assured, and undaunted even in the face of apparent disaster, because they can see beyond the present. They can look past petty defeats and setbacks. They can plot and plan far, far in advance of the day of vindication. They have a future orientation. They believe in the idea of progress.

Though that progress may come in small stages over long epochs, visionary men know that it eventually *will* come. They believe in its inevitability.

And so they toil. Day in and day out. Year in and year out. Never despising "the day of small beginnings" (Zechariah 4:10).

This is a special legacy of Christianity in Western Civilization. It was the Biblical conceptions of hope, promise, patience, assurance, victory, advance, dominion, confidence, faith and conviction that set the West on its course of cultural, technological, and sociological progress.

Sadly, that special legacy has been abandoned of late by believers and appropriated by the enemies of the faith. For more than one hundred years it has been the humanists who have utilized the Christian idea of progress to sponsor their insidious aims while believers have been culturally sequestered and emasculated by their pessimism.

For generations virtually the only visionaries this culture has known have been men like Harlan Payne—men utterly at odds with God's purposes.

**The advocates of abortion-on-demand were visionaries.** For years they worked systematically, consistently, and diligently, waiting for their day. From the 1860's on, the infamous Alice Restell labored at her task: relentlessly chipping away at the public morality, aggressively litigating in the courts, and tirelessly wooing politicians, journalists, and doctors. From the 1920's on, Restell's torch was carried by another woman of infamy, Margaret Sanger. She launched media campaigns, commissioned extensive demographic studies, pulled together vast political networks, and initiated massive re-education strategies until, at long last, her Planned Parenthood ideology was successful in implementing its "gentle genocide." Christians wouldn't begin wrestling with the abortion issue until after the 1973 Roe v. Wade decision. The visionary humanists were ahead of the game by more than a century.

**The advocates of international socialism were visionaries.** For years, they too worked systematically, consistently, and diligently, waiting for their day. From the 1830's on, the notorious Karl Marx labored at his task: mercilessly attacking the capitalist system, prolifically churning out revolutionary literature, and incessantly crafting the organizations that would herald the day of the proletariat. From the 1840's on, Marx's torch was carried by Vladimir Ulyanov (better known as Lenin). He too was fervent in his criticism, in his writing, and in his organizing. But he added his passionately incendiary dedication and his psychotically zealous temper until at long last his Bolshevik ideology was successful in redrawing the world map. Christians wouldn't begin wrestling with the Communist issue until after the Korean War in 1953. The visionary humanists were ahead of the game by more than a century.

**The advocates of sexual liberalization were visionaries.** For years, they too worked systematically, consistently, and diligently, waiting for their day. From the 1880's on, the ignoble Havelock Ellis labored at this task: unremittingly distributing pornography, remorselessly promoting promiscuity, and religiously infecting the young. From the 1940's on, Ellis' torch was carried by Alfred Kinsey. Under the guise of scientific inquiry he indulged his lusts with any and every manner of perversion, lasciviousness, and concupiscence. He pursued his abominations with vengeance: carefully mollifying them, detoxifying them, and vesting them with academic jargon until, at long last, his erotic ideology was successful in redefining human sexuality. Christians wouldn't begin wrestling with the proliferation of illicit sexual propaganda until after *Hustler* and *Penthouse* joined *Playboy* on the shelves of 7-Eleven in 1972. Again, the visionary humanists were ahead of the game by more than a century.

Likewise, the advocates of homosexuality, infanticide, pedophilia, euthanasia, and a myriad of other debaucheries have actively promoted their causes with vision and purpose, while believers have stood idly by.

Clearly, when Christians abdicate their God-given place as a nation's pioneers, as a culture's visionaries, oppression abounds and all of society suffers.

> When the wicked increase, transgression increases . . . for where there is no vision the people perish (Proverbs 29:16,18).

## All Out War

Perhaps the blessings of liberty and prosperity in Western culture have softened Christians to the point that they no longer see the cosmic dimensions of the life-and-death struggle that rages all around. Perhaps the life of relative ease and carelessness that American Christians have come to enjoy has served to blind them to the unholy war for men and nations that has erupted with fury in every corner of the globe. Perhaps their apathy, complacency, impotence, and lack of vision is the luxury of modernity.

If so, such luxury is sure to be short-lived.

The war is all too real.

The purblind cannot, and will not, survive.

If Christians are going to rebuild the walls of this culture, if they are going to help restore America's greatness, then they are going to have to reclaim their lost legacy. They are going to have to become men and women of vision. They are going to have to enter the fray.

Visionaries understand the implications of all out war. They understand the stakes. They know the risks.

That is why they take seriously the Apostle Paul's admonition to "put on the full armor of God" in order to prepare for conflict with the dastardly forces of wickedness (Ephesians 6:10-18). They understand it to be their calling to "wage war," to "demolish strongholds," and to "tear down fortresses" (2 Corinthians 10:4-5). They realize the necessity of "suffering hardship as good soldiers of Christ Jesus" (2 Timothy 2:3).

While they know that their primary enemies are not "flesh and blood" (Ephesians 6:12), and, thus, they are "not to wage war as the world does" (2 Corinthians 10:3), visionaries never lose sight of the fact that the war is very real. It is not some metaphysical, intangible, esoteric, and invisible war. It involves cultures, civilizations, institutions, powers, and principalities. It involves men and nations, not simply demons and hobgoblins.

The Bible makes this very clear. It's all out war. It's real. It's serious. It's deadly.

Opponents are disarmed (Colossians 2:15). Captives are taken (2 Corinthians 10:5). And casualties are exacted (1 Peter 5:8).

Commissions are extended (Mark 6:15). Ambassadors are engaged (2 Corinthians 5:20). Weapons are dispensed (2 Corinthians 10:4). Strategies are formulated (Revelation 5:1-8). Espionage is exposed (Acts 20:29-30). Battle cries are sounded (1 Corinthians 14:8). And victories are won (1 John 5:4).

It is not enough simply to hold to the unchanging standard of Scripture, the unwavering standard of servanthood, and the uncompromising standard of true spirituality. Christians must *focus* their belief, their service, and their character through the lens of vision. When the battles rage, the conflicts intensify, and the weariness of war sets in, it is only the passionate conviction of vision that enables belief, service, and character to persevere.

It is only the idea of progress, the future orientation, and the unnerving tenacity of undaunted vision that enlivens belief, service, and character in the day of distress.

### Empowered Faith
Belief gives faith its substance. Service then authenticates that substance, while character validates it.

But it is vision that catalyzes and empowers faith. It is vision that releases faith from the safety zone of irrelevancy into the war zone of cultural transformation.

Thus, it was only by exercising visionary faith that believers in past ages were able to "conquer kingdoms, perform acts of righteousness, obtain promises, shut the mouths of lions, quench the power of fire, escape the edge of the sword, and from weakness be made strong" (Hebrews 11:33-34).

The pattern is uniform and consistent throughout the Scriptures.

**Joseph exercised visionary faith.** He risked everything by refusing to compromise his obedience to the plans and purposes of God (Genesis 39:7-16). As a result, he suffered persecution and was even thrown into prison (Genesis 39:19-20). But Joseph's vision remained undaunted. He persevered and before long, God raised him up out of the depths to rule over the whole land (Genesis 41:37-45).

**David exercised visionary faith.** He risked everything by refusing to compromise his obedience to the plans and purposes of God (1 Samuel 18:1-16). As a result, he suffered persecution and was even cast into exile (1 Samuel 19:11-18). But David's vision remained undaunted. He persevered and, before long, God raised him up out of the depths to rule over the whole land (2 Samuel 2:4).

**Daniel exercised visionary faith.** He risked everything by refusing to compromise his obedience to the plans and purposes of God (Daniel 6:10). As a result, he too suffered persecution and was ultimately thrown into the lions' den (Daniel 6:11-16). But Daniel's vision remained undaunted. He persevered and before long, God raised him up out of the depths to rule over the whole land (Daniel 6:25-28).

**The early Christians exercised visionary faith.** They too risked everything by refusing to compromise their obedience to the plans and purposes of God (Acts 4:19-20). As a result, they suffered persecution and were even thrown into prison (Acts 5:19). But their vision remained undaunted. They persevered and, before long, God raised them up out of the depths to rule over the whole land (Acts 19:26).

Again and again the Bible verifies the overcoming vitality of visionary faith: in the story of Esther (Esther 3:6-15; 8:17), in the story of Job (Job 1:13-22; 42:10-15), in the story of Elijah (1 Kings 17:1-16; 18:20-46), in the story of Micaiah (1 Kings 22:7-12, 24-40), and in the story of the Apostle Paul (Philippians 1:7; 3:8-16). In each of these stories, the heroes of the faith were able to see *past* the most difficult and oppressive circumstances to the day of glory. They were visionaries. Thus, they were able to be persistent, consistent, and committed over the long haul. Their faith was *empowered* for the day of battle. And so they were able to transform their cultures and societies according to God's will and way.

## True Discipleship

The essence of discipleship is historical modeling: following the example of those visionary men and women who have gone before, shunning the example of the wicked. The heroes of the faith are models to be imitated (Hebrews 12:1). The villains of history are models to be avoided (1 Corinthians 15:33).

Thus, the Apostle Paul was insistent that his converts imitate him (1 Corinthians 4:6; 11:1) and follow his example (Philippians 3:17, 4:9; 1 Thessalonians 1:6; 2 Thessalonians 3:9), while at the same time shunning evil-doers (Philippians 3:2), and avoiding apostates altogether (1 Corinthians 5:11-13).

God set these examples up very purposefully. He set them up for the instruction of His people—to instill vision in them (1 Corinthians 10:1-11).

This is why history is such a crucial concern for Christians. History provides a context for their vision. It provides perspective. It gives depth to their optimism, their future orientation, and their commitment. It enables their conviction to withstand the eroding effects of battle fatigue, because it provides an objective record of vision in action.

If Christians are going to rebuild the walls of this culture, if they are going to help restore America's greatness, then they are going to have to imitate Joseph, David, Daniel, Paul, and the other heroes of the faith while simultaneously battling, resisting, and shunning the Harlan Paynes, the Margaret Sangers, the Vladimir Ulyanovs, and the Alfred Kinseys. In short, they will have to enter the fray as men and women of vision.

## Implementing Vision

Church history is filled to overflowing with such visionary men and women. They not only believed the Bible, served the needy, and walked with character, they were passionately committed to the work of God over the long haul. They fought the good fight. They confidently awaited the day of vindication.

They did not simply *have* vision, they *implemented* vision.

**Athanasius (296-373) was a true disciple.** He was a man of undaunted vision. Imitating those faithful saints who had gone before—men like Anthony of Egypt, Irenaeus of Lyons, Ignatius of Antioch, and Polycarp of Smyrna—he stood against the rising tide of impurity and complacency in the Church. He was exiled from his home in Alexandria five times by various Bishops, Lords, and Emperors. But his commitment never wavered. His confidence never waned. His convictions never dulled. And his vision never dimmed.

He stood tirelessly for the veracity of Scripture. He gave himself sacrificially to the poor and needy. His character was a sterling example of piety and devotion. But there is no question that it was his vision that set him apart, enabling him almost single-handedly to transform the culture of his day.

**Philip Neri (1515-1595) was a true disciple.** He was a man of undaunted vision. Imitating those faithful saints who had gone before—men like Jan Hus, Savonarola, and Sebastian of San Marco—he struggled to reform the Church from within by reviving the society from without. Criticized and hounded from Florence to Rome and back for his work among the convalescent sick, he was constantly on guard for his life. But his commitment never wavered. His confidence never waned. His convictions never dulled. And his vision never dimmed.

He founded Oratory Societies for the popular exposition of God's Word. He founded charity hostels, hospices, and hospitals, including the great Trinity Hospital in Rome. He modeled a life of prayer and holiness. But it was his vision that eventually propelled him into prominence and preeminence in his culture.

**Cyril Lucaris (1572-1638) was a true disciple.** He was a man of undaunted vision. Imitating those faithful saints who had gone before—men like Augustine, John Chrysostom, and John Wyclif—he battled the forces of cudulence, compromise, and complacency to his dying day. He scandalized his peers in the Eastern Orthodox Church when, acting as the Patriarch of Constantinople, he began nurturing a friendship with John

Calvin the man, and an affinity with Calvinism the theology. Though he was harassed, threatened, bullied, and scorned by Jesuits, Ottomans, and Orthodox, his commitment never wavered. His confidence never waned. His convictions never dulled. And his vision never dimmed.

He fought for the authority and primacy of the Bible for all of life. He established schools, book binderies, and almshouses. He lived a life of unquestioned integrity and uprightness. But it was his vision that stirred the waters of his culture sufficiently to bring the Reformation to the East.

Dozens of other examples of visionary men shaping and leading their cultures for Christ could be cited: Germanus of Constantinople (634-730), Peter Damian (1007-1072), Margaret of Scotland (1045-1093), Oliver Cromwell (1599-1658), and Vincent de Paul (1580-1660). The fact is, whenever and wherever Christians enter the struggle for men and nations empowered by undaunted vision they overcome obstacles, overtake impediments, and overpower strongholds. They are able to rebuild the walls and restore greatness. They are able to triumph over evil.

## Conclusion

Many Christians in America today have strong convictions about the authority of the Bible. Many others have developed a deep commitment to the needy. Still others have nurtured an abiding sensitivity to spiritual disciplines.

Together these three strains of evangelical influence have built the strongest, largest, and most conspicuous Christian presence that this nation has ever known. There are more Churches, with more money and more members, than at any other time in history.

And yet the cultural and moral decline is more drastic than ever before.

What is the missing ingredient?

Very simply, it is *vision*. And "where there is no vision the people perish" (Proverbs 29:18).

Without the commitment, confidence, and conviction of vision, the faith of American Christians has been complacent, compromised, and corpulent. It has not been able to withstand the assaults of battle with the enemies of God. It has not been able to bear up under the mantle of discipleship passed from generation to generation for the last two thousand years.

If this nation is to be turned around in any measure, this missing ingredient must be restored.

It is essential for Christians to hold to the unchanging standard of Scripture, the unwavering standard of servanthood, and the uncompromising standard of true spirituality. But it is equally essential for Christians to inculcate passionate, strident, undaunted vision.

> Therefore, do not prove unfaithful nor disobedient to the heavenly vision (Acts 26:19).

# PART THREE

# THE PLAN

Teach your sons politics and war, so that their sons may study medicine and mathematics, so that their sons may study painting, poetry, music, and architecture.

John Adams

# LAYING FOUNDATIONS

A mood of restless tension filled the room.

Tempers flared. Frustrations soared. Anxiety rose. Apprehension set in. Despair prevailed.

It was a meeting of parents. Very concerned parents. They had come together to discuss options and to formulate strategies.

But their options seemed few and far between. Their strategies were tired and impotent.

And they knew it.

"We feel so helpless," said one young father.

"It seems as if there is absolutely nothing we can do," said another.

"All the cards are stacked against us. We don't have the political pull, the connections, the resources, or the savvy to do much of anything except gripe and complain," said still another.

One speaker after another addressed the group, hoping against hope to instill some new spark of confidence.

All to no avail.

The State Board of Education, under the direction of the National Education Association, had just handed down a series of new regulations severely restricting Christian day schools and home schools. The provisions were written in such a way that there appeared to be no escape clauses, no alternative appeals, and no judicial loopholes. The humanists had done their homework and had come up with an iron clad bill. It would subject all educational programs to state control, attaching severe penalties to churches, families, and schools that failed to comply.

These parents had come together thinking that they could not stand idly by while their children's future and their families' freedom hung in the balance.

But what could they do?

Realistically?

"Oh, I suppose we could write some letters, attend some meetings, and issue some statements," said one frustrated mom. "But what good would that do? Really? They've got us by the throat. How can a few Christian families with few or no resources expect to go up against the monolithic bureaucratic blockade? I hate to just give up, but no one here has any idea of how to address these problems. Not really. And I don't know anyone who does."

"I know what's right and I know what's wrong," said another mom. "But, quite frankly, I'm getting sick and tired of hearing about how things *ought* to be, or how things *used* to be. What I want to know is how we can turn things around. I want to know what to do. I want specifics. I want a plan of action. Something more than just writing my congressman. I'm ready to go to work. I just need to know what to do. Doesn't anybody know what to do?"

Sadly, these parents' cry of frustration has been echoed all across the nation, again and again, as the well-greased machine of the humanistic juggernaut has rolled mercilessly over life and liberty, hope and happiness. With the vast resources of industry, banking, education, media, and government thrown fully behind that awful, awesome machine, what hope does a small contingent of Christians have of stopping its draconian assault?

What can they do?

Realistically?

### The Nehemiah Paradigm

These were the kinds of questions Nehemiah must have been asking himself shortly after receiving reports of Jerusalem's demise.

The walls of the city — symbols of her strength — had been reduced to rubble. The gates of the city — symbols of her security — had been burned to ash. And all the world stood opposed to their restoration.

The people of the city were frustrated, fearful and despondent. They were entirely bereft of the power, the resources, the skills, or even the incentive to do anything.

Nehemiah understood that the odds were stacked against

him. He understood the risks. But he didn't cave in to the oppression of circumstance or the tyranny of appearances. He knew that *with God there is always a way.*

Nothing is impossible with God (Philippians 4:13). He can move mountains for His people (Mark 11:23). He can change hearts (Proverbs 21:1). He can multiply resources (1 King 17:14-16). He can transform circumstances (James 5:16-18).

And He will.

And He does.

> For the Lord God is a sun and shield; The Lord will give grace and glory; No good thing will He withhold from those who walk uprightly (Psalm 84:11).

> Every good gift and every perfect gift is from above, and comes down from the Father of lights, with whom there is no variation or shadow of turning (James 1:17).

He gives overcoming courage, strength, help, and victory (Isaiah 41:1-20). He gives direction (Psalm 5:8). He establishes plans (Proverbs 16:3). He confirms work (Psalm 90:17). And He rewards those who diligently seek Him (Hebrews 11:6).

By faith, the people of God can snatch victory out of the snarling jaws of defeat (Romans 8:28). They have been made "more than conquerors" (Romans 8:37) and "overcomers" (1 John 5:4) by His grace.

Nehemiah knew that.

He also knew that "the noble man devises noble plans. And by noble plans he stands" (Isaiah 32:8). So he began to plan. Against all odds. He began to lay the foundations of victory. In the face of the impossible.

And what were those plans? What kind of foundations did he lay?

Very simply, they were: intercession followed by information, involvement, investment, and implementation.

If Christians in this day of humanistic tyranny and circumstantial hopelessness are to begin to rebuild the walls of American culture, and to restore its lost greatness, they had best pay heed to the Nehemiah paradigm.

They are going to have to establish their belief in the Bible,

their service to man, their faultless character, and their undaunted vision. And they are going to have to establish them
with solid, tangible, workable, godly *plans*. Nehemiah-like
plans.

### Intercession

Prayer changes things.

No matter how bad things may look, no matter how ominously the odds may be stacked against the cause of truth, prayer
can turn it all around.

The humanists may have a frightening advantage in money
and manpower. They may have unending resources and unflagging energy. But Christians have prayer.

And prayer is the most potent force in all the cosmos availed
to mere mortal men.

That is why the Bible makes it plain that Christians are to be
*constant* in prayer.

They are to pray in the morning (Mark 1:35). They are to
pray at noon (Psalm 55:17). They are to pray in the evening
(Mark 6:46). They are to pray during the night watch (Luke
6:12). In fact, they are to pray unceasingly (1 Thessalonians 5:17).

God has given Christians access to His throne (Hebrews
4:16). He has given them fellowship with Christ (1 Corinthians
1:9), and counsel with the Holy Spirit (John 14:26). Therefore,
they are to make use of the glorious privilege of prayer at *every
opportunity* (1 Timothy 2:8).

When Nehemiah began to make his plans, when he began to
lay the foundations for victory in Jerusalem, he first fell to his
knees in prayer.

He knew that in order to solve the impossibly complex political crisis at hand, he would have to exercise a great deal of political savvy, and call in all his political options. He knew he would
have to win the King's favor (Nehemiah 1:11), obtain the King's
blessing (Nehemiah 2:1-5), and make use of the King's resources
(Nehemiah 2:6-9).

But before he could do any of that, he would have to pray.
And so he did.

For an entire month Nehemiah did nothing but pray
(Nehemiah 1:1; 2:1).

Even after his plans began to take shape, Nehemiah was *constant* in intercession. When he petitioned the King to allow him to rebuild the walls of Jerusalem, he prayed (Nehemiah 2:4). When he entered the ruined city to begin the task, he prayed (Nehemiah 2:12). When he was met with opposition and persecution, he prayed (Nehemiah 4:2). When conflicts arose among the workers, he prayed (Nehemiah 5:19). When violence, conspiracy, espionage, and corruption jeopardized the project, he prayed (Nehemiah 4:2). He didn't panic. He didn't despair. He didn't give up or give in. He prayed (Nehemiah 6:9, 14).

Throughout all the ups and downs, the political set backs, the physical obstacles, and the spiritual trials, Nehemiah was able to remain steadfast. He was confident that God would give him success (Nehemiah 2:20). He was sure God would endow him with strength (Nehemiah 6:9), show him gracious favor (Nehemiah 2:18), and see him through to the end (Nehemiah 2:12). He was unwavering in his optimism because the entire project had been conceived and confirmed in prayer (Nehemiah 7:5).

There was no way he could fail. No matter what the odds.

What was true for Nehemiah then, is just as true for Christians now.

Prayer changes things.

Even when things are at their worst.

Prayer binds and it looses (Matthew 18:18). It casts down and it raises up (Mark 11:23-24). It ushers in peace (1 Timothy 2:1-2), forgiveness (Mark 11:25), healing (James 5:14-15), liberty (2 Corinthians 3:17), wisdom (1 Kings 3:3-14), and protection (Psalm 41:2).

If Christians are going to rebuild the walls of this culture, if they are going to help restore America's greatness, they are going to have to pray. They are going to have to pray with wholeheartedness (Jeremiah 29:13). They are going to have to pray with contrition (2 Chronicles 7:14). They are going to have to pray faithfully (Mark 11:24), fervently (James 5:16), obediently (1 John 3:22), and confidently (John 15:7).

If Christians really want to know *what to do*, if they really want a *plan*, if they really want to *lay the foundations* for victory, here's the place to start: prayer.

**First, Christians need to develop personal prayer disci-**

**plines**. They need to pray for national and cultural revival. They need to intercede mightily and persistently for their magistrates and leaders. They need to be specific: naming names, stating issues, claiming promises, and invoking Scripture. They need to cry out from their prayer closets for justice and mercy to blanket the land like a sweet morning dew.

**Second, Christians need to develop corporate prayer disciplines**. They need to infuse Church worship with the unction and gumption that can only come by fervent intercession. They need to pray corporate benediction and blessing for those who honor God's Word in the cultural and civil spheres (Psalm 69:13-19). And they need to pray malediction and cursing for those who impugn God's Word in the cultural and civil spheres (Psalm 69:20-28). The practice of singing Approbative Psalms (hymns of blessing from the Psalter: 5, 7, 9, 20, 23, 25, 65, 75, 113, etc.) and Imprecatory Psalms (hymns of cursing from the Psalter: 2, 10, 35, 55, 69, 79, 83, 94, 109, 140, etc.) has long been the first recourse of political and cultural influence for the Church.

**Third, Christians need to develop local prayer hotlines**. They need to be able to respond quickly and decisively to the various machinations of the humanistic juggernaut. They need to be able to lift one another's burdens (Galatians 6:2). They need to be able to respond to the trumpet call (Joshua 2:15). They need to be able to sound the alarms (Amos 3:6).

**Fourth, Christians need to develop national prayer networks**. Where a phone tree may work on the local level, national issues, circumstances, and events require a more comprehensive plan. Newsletters such as the ones put out by *Intercessors for America*, *Focus on the Family*, and *The Christian Action Council*, or radio broadcasts such as *Contact America*, *The Christian Worldview*, and *Point of View* provide the coverage, the flexibility, the accuracy, and the speed that are essential for effectual prayer. Computer billboards, satellite link-ups, and short wave skip beams can also be utilized for this purpose. The point is, Christians need to utilize every possible resource and pursue every possible avenue to spark a national prayer revival of monumental proportions.

If Christians really want to know *what to do*, if they really want a *plan*, if they really want to *lay the foundations* for victory, this is the place to start.

## Information

Christians need to know what is going on.

Knowledge makes things happen.

"If we could just get the word out to folks about what is *really* going on," one concerned parent asserted, "I don't think the humanists would have a hope of a chance."

In the same meeting, another parent stated "Most people I know would be shocked beyond belief if they ever found out what's really going on in our schools, at places like Planned Parenthood, and all the other humanist dens of iniquity. We've got to find a way of confirming and distributing this knowledge."

The Bible says that "through knowledge the righteous are delivered" (Proverbs 11:9), but they are "exiled for the lack of knowledge" (Isaiah 5:13).

If knowledge of the truth does not proliferate, a society is doomed. Since only Christians have the motivation to promote such knowledge, they will have to take on that burden. They can't depend on the educational system. They can't depend on the established media. They can't depend on government studies, surveys, or investigations. They will have to do the work themselves.

The fact is, "the senseless *have no* knowledge" (Psalm 92:6), "fools *shun* knowledge" (Proverbs 1:22), while "the ungodly *hate* knowledge" (Proverbs 1:29). If Christians don't actively disseminate accurate information about what is going on in this culture *no one will.*

This is why the Bible makes it plain that Christians are to devote themselves to the information business.

Knowledge makes things happen.

Thus, they are to seek knowledge (Proverbs 8:10). They are to store it up (Proverbs 10:14). And they are to preserve it (Malachi 2:7). They are to apply their minds to know it (Proverbs 22:17). They are to apply their hearts to receive it (Proverbs 23:12). And they are to apply their lives to spread it (Proverbs 15:7).

When Nehemiah began to make his plans, when he began to lay the foundations for victory in Jerusalem, he immediately began to gather and to disseminate information.

He knew that in order to restore the city's dignity he would have to work hard (Nehemiah 5:16), organize well (Nehemiah 3:1-32), and manage effectively (Nehemiah 13:4-30).

But before he could do any of that he would have to gain knowledge.

And so he did.

He gathered information from eyewitnesses (Nehemiah 1:2-4). He made inquiry of the King (Nehemiah 2:5). He made contacts concerning resource procurement (Nehemiah 2:6-8). He made personal assessments (Nehemiah 2:11-16).

And then he made public disclosures (Nehemiah 2:17-20).

Nehemiah did his homework. He confirmed his facts, separating truth from rumor, and then he got those facts before the people (Nehemiah 4:14) and the authorities (Nehemiah 5:14-18).

Nehemiah was a man of prayer. But he did not live with his head in the clouds. His intimate relationship with God drove him to be a man of knowledge and wisdom (Exodus 31:30), for "the Lord is a God of knowledge" (1 Samuel 2:3), and "the fear of the Lord is the beginning of knowledge" (Proverbs 1:7).

What was true for Nehemiah then should be just as true for Christians today.

A nation is "destroyed for a lack of knowledge" (Hosea 4:6).

If Christians don't collect, verify, and provide the information about the insidious plans and programs of the National Organization for Women, the People for the American Way, Planned Parenthood, the American Civil Liberties Union, the National Education Association, the Council on Foreign Relations, the Internal Revenue Service, the Trilateral Commission, *et al*, no one will, and this culture will be extinguished.

Knowledge makes things happen.

It produces endurance (Proverbs 28:2). It multiplies resources (Proverbs 24:4). It provides encouragement (Proverbs 2:10). It releases power (Proverbs 24:5), joy (Ecclesiastes 2:26), prudence (Proverbs 13:16), and security (Ecclesiastes 7:12).

If Christians are going to rebuild the walls of this culture, if they are going to help restore America's greatness, they are going to have to become conduits of information. They are going to have to get the word out. They are going to have to get their facts and figures straight and then communicate those facts and figures effectively.

If Christians really want to know *what to do*, if they really want a *plan*, if they really want to *lay the foundations* for victory, here's the next step: inform the people.

**First, Christians need to develop personal study and communication disciplines.** If they want to lead then they'll have to *read.* They need to read books, magazines, tracts, newsletters, journals, monographs, and newspapers. And if they read, then they'll need to *lead.* With knowledge comes responsibility. They need to teach Sunday School classes in the area of their expertise, print up a small circulation newsletter for their neighborhood or Church, teach an extension class at the local community college, write letters to the editor, and conduct home Bible studies or issue oriented discussions. They need to learn the facts and then they need to get those facts widely disseminated.

**Second, Christians need to develop local information networks.** Whenever a development occurs in the legislature, or in the bond market, or in the schools, or in the media, a local network needs to swing into motion. Telephone trees, xeroxed notices, computer bulletins, cable TV flashes, radio announcements, newsletter distribution, and direct mail drops can be utilized if the network has been set up ahead of time.

**Third, Christians need to develop local Church information centers.** The Church should be the locus of healing, hope, wisdom, and knowledge. Sunday bulletins, Church newsletters, local radio programming, bulletin boards, special Sunday School classes, and announcements from the pulpit can, and should, be utilized to distribute accurate information about cultural, political, spiritual, and societal goings on. The Church should be relevant and vital to the issues of the day. Only then can she be all that God has called her to be.

**Fourth, Christians need to develop national information networks.** This is the information age. So not only is there a proliferation of information, but there is also a proliferation of information technologies. Sadly, Christians have failed to capitalize on those new technologies. But of course one or two brave pioneers could quickly and easily turn things around. For instance, the *Contact America* radio broadcast has quickly become a national focus, hi-tech, data distribution system. Not only are

there daily updates of executive, legislative, judicial, and bureaucratic actions on the call-in portion of the program, but
there is under development a comprehensive computer network
reaching into every one of the four-hundred thirty-five congressional districts nationwide. This network would provide instantaneous reporting of significant developments. One congressman said of *Contact America's* plan "This is every representative's
nightmare: the people back home aware of every move we
make." The plan, which is already partially deployed, will not
only create an accountability never before possible, or even imaginable, but will put the reins of government back into the
hands of the people—where it belongs in the first place.

If Christians really want to know *what to do*, if they really
want a *plan*, if they really want to *lay the foundations* for victory,
here's the next step: inform the people.

### Involvement

The masses must be mobilized.

It is not enough simply to pray and inform, people must be
mobilized to take action. They must be recruited for the cause of
truth. They must be motivated to act on the truth. They must be
equipped to fight for the truth.

The key to winning a culture is *not* to assault the palaces. It is
to capture the countryside.

Christians need to get people involved.

They need to realize that the evangelistic task does not end at
the moment of salvation, but follows a convert through to full
and mature discipleship (Matthew 28:19-20). It includes teaching, training, encouraging, developing, motivating, mobilizing,
and involving (Ephesians 4:11-16).

That is why the Bible puts such a heavy emphasis on body
life and mutual ministry. *All* Christians are to put their hands to
the plow, do the work of the ministry, and contribute to
Kingdom service. *Every single believer* has received the call.

Since they are called, it is essential that they be involved.
And since they are to be involved, other Christians are to provoke such involvement (Hebrews 10:24-25).

Thus, Christians are to "encourage one another" (1 Thessalonians 5:11). They are to "serve one another" (Galatians 5:13).

They are to "provoke one another" (Colossians 3:16), "admonish one another" (Romans 15:14), and "edify one another" (Romans 15:7).

In so nurturing the community of faith, Christians are able to not only pray for workers (Matthew 9:37-38), and preach for workers (Matthew 10:7), they are also able to train up workers (2 Timothy 2:2). They are able to recruit from the ranks.

When Nehemiah began to make his plans, when he began to lay the foundations for victory in Jerusalem, he immediately began to involve others.

He knew that in order to accomplish the task before him he would have to do much himself: planning (Nehemiah 2:7-8), working (Nehemiah 4:23), sacrificing (Nehemiah 4:14-19), adjusting (Nehemiah 2:19-20), and improvising (Nehemiah 4:21-23).

But before he could do any of that, he would have to involve others.

And so he did.

He went to the people and enlisted qualified help (Nehemiah 2:9). He then encouraged those workers (Nehemiah 2:17-18). He motivated them (Nehemiah 4:14-20). He organized them, delegating the various tasks (Nehemiah 3:1-32). He even anticipated difficulties with them and made provisions for them (Nehemiah 6:1-14).

Nehemiah never stood alone. His work was built around the gifts, the abilities, the stewardship, and the commitment of the entire community.

What was true for Nehemiah then should be just as true for Christians today.

> Now there are diversities of gifts, but the same Spirit. There are differences of ministries, but the same Lord. And there are diversities of activities, but it is the same God who works all in all. But the manifestation of the Spirit is given to each one for the profit of all. For in fact the body is not one member but many (1 Corinthians 12:4-7, 14).

Coordination and unity are not only sweet and soothing (Psalm 133:1-3), they also pave the way for peace (Romans 14:19), steadfastness (Philippians 1:27), and joy (Philippians 2:2). The fact is when men work together in harmony, singlemindedness, and unity "nothing can be withheld from them" (Genesis 11:1-6).

If Christians are going to rebuild the walls of this culture, if they are going to help restore America's greatness, they are going to have to solicit widespread involvement from the entire community of faith. They are going to have to mobilize the masses. They are going to have to get the Church motivated and activated. They are going to have to enlist, recruit, train, delegate, muster, catalyze, and commission the forces.

If Christians really want to know *what to do*, if they really want to *plan*, if they really want to *lay the foundations* for victory, here's the next step: involve the *whole* body of Christ.

**First, Christians need to develop habits of personal evangelism, discipleship, and enlistment.** Christ has commissioned *all* His followers to become "fishers of men" (Matthew 4:19). They should *constantly* share the Gospel with the lost (Colossians 4:5). They should *constantly* build up the saved (Colossians 3:16-17). And they should *constantly* spur on the inactive (Hebrews 10:24-25). At work, at home, at Church, at school, around the neighborhood, with family members, with friends, and with casual acquaintances, Christians should be incessantly enlisting men for the Kingdom and the work of the Kingdom.

**Second, Christians need to develop community wide leadership recruitment and training programs.** Find the willing. Train the eager. Encourage the hesitant. Scour the hedgerows and beat the bushes (Luke 14:21-23). Match their duties to their gifts. Reach into the Churches, onto the campuses, and out through the radio stations. The fields are "white unto harvest." So the workers must be immediately dispatched (Matthew 9:37-38). They are needed to man phone banks, to staff counseling and relief centers, to coordinate voter registration drives, to stuff envelopes, to run computer programs, to write newsletters, to activate phone trees, to distribute press releases, to develop curriculums, to create graphics, to shuttle speakers, to operate sound and lighting, to photograph events, to research issues, (and so forth, and so on). Clearly, they are needed.

**Third, Christians need to promote and support youngsters who must be trained for the fight.** Scholarships must be secured for promising Christian students in journalism, economics, political science, computer programming, physics, engineering, literature, mathematics, philosophy, history, biology, education, fine arts, communications, chemistry, architecture, and business. And support must be developed for those few institutions that are actually taking those young impressionable students and turning them into champions for Christ, activists for the Kingdom, and workers for truth.

**Fourth, Christians need to transform their Churches into hives of activity.** Where should the picketers at the local aborturary be enlisted, trained, and mobilized? Why, the Church of course. Where should the parents learn how to educate their children? Again, the Church. Where should families learn how to care for the needy, to fight neighborhood pornography, to write to congressmen, to testify before steering committees, or to witness to a neighbor? In each case, they should learn these things at Church. In their Sunday School classes, during special seminars, at task force meetings, and from the pulpit, they should be equipped to do the *whole* work of the ministry (Ephesians 4:12).

If Christians really want to know *what to do*, if they really want a *plan*, if they really want to *lay the foundations* for victory, here's the next step: involve the *whole* body of Christ.

### Investment

You can't fight something with nothing.

And to put together something substantial you need money.

The humanists have invested vast sums of money in their dastardly programs. They have marshalled tremendous resource pools. They have funded, subsidized, and capitalized for maximum impact. They have withheld nothing from the cause.

But wealth is a gift from God, set aside for one purpose and one purpose only: to confirm the Covenant and to establish the Kingdom (Deuteronomy 8:18). Even the wealth of the wicked will one day be converted to Kingdom purposes (Proverbs 13:22).

That is why the Bible places so much emphasis on stewardship.

Every Christian should be a giver (Deuteronomy 16:17). They should give to the Church through tithes (Malachi 3:10). They should give to special projects through offerings (1 Corinthians 16:1-2). And they should give to those who have ministered to them through gifts (Galatians 6:6).

Giving is an aspect of worship (Deuteronomy 16:10-11). Thus it should be done with a cheerful heart (2 Corinthians 9:7), whether out of prosperity (1 Corinthians 16:2), or paucity (2 Corinthians 8:2).

Giving is an investment in the Kingdom of God (Matthew 6:19-21).

When Nehemiah began to make his plans, when he began to lay the foundations for victory in Jerusalem, he immediately invested in the work himself.

He knew that the task before him was a geo-political hot potato (Nehemiah 4:1-21). He knew that it was also a complex of sociological, cultural, and architectural dilemmas (Nehemiah 2:11-20).

But before he could deal with any of those problems, he would have to come up with the resources to rebuild the walls.

And so he did.

He invested time (Nehemiah 2:4-6). He invested money (Nehemiah 5:14-16). He invested resources (Nehemiah 5:17-18). He invested his very life (Nehemiah 6:1-14).

He also solicited additional help from the King (Nehemiah 2:4-5), from the governors (Nehemiah 2:7), from provincial bureaucrats (Nehemiah 2:8), and from the general citizenry (Nehemiah 3:1-32).

Of course, his use of the resources was held accountable to the King, open to his inspection (Nehemiah 2:6).

By the time he actually began the work of reconstruction, Nehemiah had accumulated only a scant few resources. But what little giving he had provoked was enough. Extravagance was entirely unnecessary. Stewardship was all that was needed.

What was true for Nehemiah then should be equally true for Christians today.

Even when in short supply, godly stewardship is able to supply needs (2 Corinthians 9:12), redeem time (Ephesians 5:16), multiply resources (2 Corinthians 9:10), and refresh the saints (Proverbs 11:24-25).

If Christians are going to rebuild the walls of this culture, if they are going to help restore America's greatness, they are going to have to develop stalwart standards of stewardship. They are going to have to put their money where their faith is.

If Christians really want to know *what to do*, if they really want a *plan*, if they really want to *lay the foundations* for victory, here's the next step: invest in the work of the Kingdom.

**First, Christians need to put their individual financial houses in order.** They need to begin to practice proper stewardship by exercising providence, thrift, and generosity. They need to apply Biblical principles of resource management: budgeting (Luke 14, 16), saving (Proverbs 6), goal setting (Proverbs 1), investment (Matthew 21), debt eradication (Romans 13:8), and of course, the tithe (Malachi 3:8-12). Only then will they have the resources nurtured and available for the battle against inhuman humanism.

**Second, Christians need to support the causes and ministries that are really accomplishing something.** The scandalous goings on in TV evangelism have only served to underscore the need to be careful in targeting our giving. Ministries that are little more than fund raising operations should be avoided at all costs. Causes that do little more than stoke the star-maker machinery of evangelicalism or politics or social action are worse than worthless. Time, resources, and money are in precious short supply. They should be carefully distributed only to those works that actually work.

**Third, Christians need to think, and give, and spend in terms of the long haul.** Political campaigns require millions of dollars. Media campaigns require millions more. Educational campaigns require still many millions more. There is no such thing as a free lunch. Cultural conquest will not come cheap or easy. Christians are going to have to plan ahead. Building coffers for a governor's race four years ahead of election day is not too soon. Developing trusts, endowments, foundations, and annuity programs is not too far-sighted. Saving by slow increments for a film project, or a philanthropic agency, or a lobbying effort is not too ambitious. It is only reasonable.

**Fourth, Christians need to realize that war-time sacrifices may be necessary.** The game of catch up is an extremely costly game to play. With the humanists ahead of Christians by nearly a century on nearly every count, it is to be expected that the effort over the next ten years will require extra exertion, extra giving, and extra sacrifice in order to catch up. The pro-life movement has to start practically from scratch. And that's expensive. The Biblical charity movement has to start practically from scratch. And that's expensive. Christians who are pioneering work in telecommunications, radio networking, computer link ups, satellite broadcasting, literature publication, agency lobbying, grassroots organizing, and a myriad of other works are facing extremely expensive propositions. It is essential that the Christian community find ways to finance each of these works.

If Christians really want to know *what to do*, if they really want a *plan*, if they really want to *lay the foundations* for victory, here's the next step: invest in the work of the Kingdom.

## Implementation

Talk is cheap.

Even the best of plans, if left unexecuted, are just empty talk.

Prayer, knowledge, recruitment, and resources without *action* can accomplish precious little.

Christians must put feet to their prayers, hands to their knowledge, commitment to their recruitment, and purpose to their resources. That is where the rubber meets the road.

And that is why the Bible puts such a heavy emphasis on actually living and doing the Christian life as opposed simply to talking about it.

> Do not merely listen to the Word, and so deceive yourselves: Do what it says. Anyone who listens to the Word but does not do what it says is like a man who looks at his face in a mirror and, after looking at himself, goes away and immediately forgets what he looks like. But the man who looks intently into the perfect Law that gives freedom, and continues to do this, not forgetting what he has heard, but doing it-he will be blessed in what he does (James 1:22-25).

> But He said, "More than that, blessed are those who hear the Word of God and keep it" (Luke 11:28).

Godly action is an exercise of true wisdom (Matthew 7:24). It affords believers blessing (John 13:17), security (Luke 6:48), and justice (Romans 2:13).

To refrain from action, however, is foolish (Matthew 7:26), hypocritical (Luke 6:46), and insecure (Matthew 7:27).

When Nehemiah began to make his plans, when he began to lay the foundations for victory in Jerusalem, he immediately set about the task of implementation.

He didn't sit on his plans.

He went right to work.

Though he had to deal with the King (Nehemiah 2:1-4), provincial governors (Nehemiah 2:7,9), imperial bureaucrats (Nehemiah 2:8), and a jealous opposition (Nehemiah 2:19), he took to his work with a vengeance. Though he had little or no resources (Nehemiah 2:12-17; 4:2), little or no experience (Nehemiah 3:1-32; 4:2), and little or no security (Nehemiah 4:7-23), he did not hesitate in the least to go forward with his task. In less than two months time, he had been able to transform a smoldering pile of rubble and ruin into a secure wall encircling all of Jerusalem (Nehemiah 6:15-16).

His plan included intercession, information, involvement, and investment, but it wasn't until he had pushed it through the implementation process that its real genius was revealed.

What was true for Nehemiah then should be equally true for Christians today.

Execution is of the essence of change. Wishing, hoping, dreaming, and scheming just won't make it happen.

If Christians are going to rebuild the walls of this culture, if they are going to help restore America's greatness, they are going to have to swing into action. They are going to have to "do the Word" (James 1:22).

> Therefore whoever hears these sayings of Mine, and does them, I will liken him to a wise man who built his house on the rock: and the rain descended, the floods came, and the winds blew and beat on that house; and it did not fall, for it was founded on the rock. Now everyone who hears these sayings of Mine, and does not do them, will be like a foolish man who built his house on the sand: and the rain descended, the floods came, and the winds blew and beat on that house; and it fell. And great was its fall (Matthew 7:24-27).

If Christians really want to know *what* to do, if they really want *a plan*, if they really want to *lay the foundations* for victory, here's the next step: implement God's principles, programs, plans, and priorities.

**First, Christians need to develop a personal program of obedience.** They need to show an individual willingness to implement God's plan for marriage, child-rearing, financial responsibility, business integrity, interpersonal ethics, and moral uprightness. They need to show themselves faithful in the small things before God can give them responsibility over the big things (Luke 16:10). They need to demonstrate that God's way and will can work in their own backyard before they impose them in someone else's backyard.

**Second, Christians need to develop local task force groups.** They need to take Christian action out of the realm of the theoretical and thrust it into the realm of the practical. They need to target specific projects and see them through to completion; win back the City Council from the humanists, eliminate pornography from the convenience stores, shut down the abortion clinics, stymie efforts to install school based sex clinics, establish an alternative to federal welfare programs, restore objectivity and accountability to news reporting, and expose local incursions by the ACLU, NOW, or the NEA.

**Third, Christians need to keep the humanists off guard.** Any good army will always display four characteristics: adaptability, unpredictability, harmony, and rapidity. The enemy never knows what to expect next. They don't know where the next blow will come from. Sadly, most Christian responses to the humanistic juggernaut have been hampered by slowness, imprecision, predictability, and disunity. Success will only come as they begin to nurture quick strike capabilities and tactical creativity.

**Fourth, Christians need to screw up the courage to act decisively.** They need to learn to "go with what they've got." Perfect conditions never come. Perfect opportunities never arrive. Successes are never guaranteed. Nothing is iron clad and secure in this poor fallen world. But Christians have a mandate to act despite the odds. They have been commissioned to stand in the gap and fight the fight no matter what.

And so they must.

If Christians really want to know *what to do*, if they really want a *plan*, if they really want to *lay the foundations* for victory, here's the next step: take action. Now.

## Conclusion

Most Christians know that something must be done to stop the slide of this culture into moral oblivion.

But what?

Where do they start? What is the plan? Who can show the way?

Although he offers no magic wand and no simple solutions, Nehemiah does answer those questions. In fact, the story of his life is an answer to those questions. His example is a model or a paradigm for Christian social action.

So what is this plan, this model, this paradigm?

First, Nehemiah prayed. He invoked the power of Almighty God.

Second, Nehemiah gathered and disseminated information. He got the facts out.

Third, Nehemiah got the whole community of faith involved. He did rank and file recruitment and leadership development.

Fourth, Nehemiah raised money. Through capital development and personal investment he scrounged together the necessary resources for the job.

And finally, Nehemiah implemented his plans. He didn't sit on his dreams. He made them come true.

Intercession, information, involvement, investment, and implementation. Now that's a plan.

In and of itself that plan does not restore a nation's greatness. But it lays the foundations for that restoration.

# EIGHT

# BEARING FRUIT

Most humanists know how to drive the car. They just don't know which way to go.

Most Christians know the way. They just can't drive the car.

It seems that life in modern times is an *either-or* situation.

*Either* we careen madly toward destruction at breakneck speeds, *or* we idle the time away, watching the world go by.

But if America's greatness is to be restored in any measure, that *either-or* situation will have to be replaced by a *both-and* situation.

*Both* heading in the right direction, *and* operating the machinery properly. *Both* knowing the way, *and* driving the car.

Dr. Steven Hovda knows the way. He has a good understanding of the Biblical principles of law, government, and society. He has laid firm foundations of intercession, information, involvement, investment, and implementation.

Now he's ready for some results. He's ready for fruit.

"We've labored for years just to get this far," he said. "We've put together a fairly strong community coalition. We've got a good set of priorities. We've got ambitious plans. We've got serious workers, sufficient resources, and specific projects. What we don't have are any *victories*. The fact is we've failed to garner any respect from those who hold public office and as a result, we've yet to bear any fruit."

Dr. Hovda's group had been able to get several referendum issues on the local ballot. They had been able to control a few select precincts. They had been able to glut the local newspaper's editorial office with letters and op-ed pieces. They had conducted a number of effective pickets on pornographic establishments and abortuaries.

"We've established a high public profile and we've established a high public awareness. But our goal is not now, nor has it ever been, *equal time for Jesus.* We want to see real and substantial *changes.* We want our labors to bear *fruit."*

The problem is that though Dr. Hovda and his fellow-workers know the way, they just haven't learned to drive the car yet. They've been sitting in the back of humanism's bus for so long that they have not developed the practical skills necessary to run the machinery of law, government, and society.

Clearly, if Christians are going to gain the influence to change this culture they are going to have to develop those practical skills. They are going to have to complement their intercession, information, involvement, investment, and implementation with disciplined cultural ability. They are going to have to *build* upon the foundations of character, vision, and passion in order to bear fruit.

In short, Christians are going to have to learn the *mechanics* of political influence. They are going to have to learn how to make the wheels of change turn in local government, in the national legislature, in the executive branch, in the courts, and in the bureaucracy. They are going to have to learn how to *get results.*

### Influencing Local Government

Local governments are the nuts and bolts of the American system. Without the administration of cities, counties, parishes, districts, precincts, zones, commissions, municipalities, and states, civil stability would utterly disintegrate. The Constitutional framers recognized that, and the governmental apparatus they designed was thus purposefully decentralized and localized. They wanted to make certain that the villages, townships, communities, and states shaped the policies of the nation and the priorities in Washington, not vice versa.

Napoleon once asserted that the way to capture a nation is not to "storm the palaces" but to "capture the countryside." He was right.

Christians, in their zeal to enter into the national political arena, have nearly forgotten the tremendous power of grassroots influence. The struggle over pornographic regulation, educational integrity, bio-medical ethics, and media accountability is not so much a matter of effecting the right legislation or appearing in the right courtroom as it is of enforcing the right zoning codes or conducting the right hearing process. By neglecting these small and seemingly insignificant matters, Christians are unable to make any headway whatsoever at the higher levels of governance.

There is a basic principle at work here—not just an American Constitutional principle but a Biblical principle—that whoever will be faithful with "few things" and "small things" will be made master over "many things" and "great things" (Matthew 25:14-30; Luke 16:10; Luke 19:12-27).

Clearly, if Christians are going to help restore America's greatness they are going to have to learn the mechanics of local government. They are going to have to familiarize themselves with the processes of community affairs, and then involve themselves in those processes.

There are several places to start: local meetings, precinct caucuses, and election campaigns.

**By attending local meetings Christians can magnify their influence and impact a hundred-fold or more.** School Board meetings, Utility District meetings, City Council meetings, County Development meetings, Environmental Impact Assessment meetings, and Tax Appraisal meetings determine the course of community life. But only a tiny handful of people—about one-tenth of 1% of the registered voters—attend those meetings on a *regular* basis. Only about 2 percent of the electorate *ever* attend such meetings. Needless to say, that minuscule minority has an inordinate amount of influence over the day to day administration of their local governing bodies.

More significant even than casting a ballot on election day is testimony before a hearing committee, or a deposition before a regulatory commission, or a statement before a council session, or a declaration before a grange conference. Christians need to attend these meetings. They need to look, listen, and learn. They need to gather facts, develop alternatives, formulate strategies, investigate possibilities, and challenge conventions. They need to speak up and speak out. They need to sit on committees, offer their services, and utilize their expertise. They need to get to know their magistrates and hold them accountable.

If a Christian presence is never felt by local leaders, if the status quo of humanism is never questioned at the city, county, or state levels, then there is little hope that the walls of this nation can be rebuilt. Christians therefore need to learn the mechanics of local assemblies. They need to bear fruit.

**By participating in precinct caucuses Christians can fundamentally alter the shape of partisan politics.** The precinct is the lowest common denominator in the American political process. Very simply, it is the election district. The precinct is the place where votes are cast and counted.

But the precinct is also the hub of party organization. It is there in the precinct caucus that the Republican, Democratic, Libertarian, and all the other political parties receive their direction, support, continuity, platform, and purpose. What a party is, whom it nominates, and where it is going is determined in those small meetings all across the country in schools, American Legion halls, and polling booths, *not* under the bright lights of television oglers in vast urban convention centers.

Every person who votes in a party's primary is eligible to participate in those all important caucuses. But only about 3 percent actually do. Very few of that tiny percentage are committed Christians. The humanists are quite happy to fill that void. Is it any wonder then that Christian concerns are almost totally unrepresented in the platforms of the major political parties?

Christians need to participate in their local caucuses. They need to submit resolutions to be adopted into the platforms. They need to elect their own precinct chairmen, election marshals, poll watchers, and convention delegates. They need to learn the rules, play the game, and determine the outcome.

If a Christian presence is never felt on the precinct level, if the strangle hold of humanism on the major parties is not confronted head-on, there is little hope that the walls of this nation can be rebuilt. Christians therefore need to learn the mechanics of the precinct caucus. They need to bear fruit.

**By actively campaigning and turning out the vote Christians can dramatically effect the direction of American culture and policy.** Every vote matters. In 1960, John F. Kennedy defeated Richard Nixon for the presidency by fewer than one vote per precinct. The "landslide" victory of Lyndon Johnson over Barry Goldwater in 1964 involved less than three votes per precinct. The fact is, never once in the history of our nation has a *majority* of the citizens elected a president. Just 26.7 percent of the electorate put Ronald Reagan in the White House in 1980's "conservative sweep." And a mere 32.3 percent helped him "swamp" the Democratic ticket in 1984.

Since only about 60 percent of the citizens of this country are registered to vote and only about 35 percent actually bother to go to the polls, a candidate only needs to get the support of a small, elite group of people to win. It only takes about 14 percent of the electorate to gain a seat in the Senate. It takes about 11 percent to gain a seat in the House. Only about 9 percent is needed to win a governorship. And it takes a mere 7 percent to take an average mayoral or city council post.

Even with all their media support, financial resources, institutional connections, industrial backing, and national exposure, humanist candidates can be defeated by a handful of well organized, well informed, and dedicated Christians.

Christians need to get involved in worthy campaigns. They need to stuff envelopes, post yard signs, distribute bumper stickers, man phone banks, hold coffee-klatches, call community meetings, and host candidate forums. They need to mount organized voter registration drives in Churches and community associations. They need to coordinate election day turn-out activities. In short, they need to make every vote count in the right column.

After all, every vote matters.

If a Christian presence is never felt at election time, if the humanistic establishment is not challenged at the polls, there is little hope that the walls of this culture can be rebuilt. Christians therefore need to learn the mechanics of political campaigns. They need to bear fruit.

Local meetings, precinct caucuses, and election campaigns: these are the keys to influencing local government. And influencing local government is the first step toward restoring America's greatness.

### Influencing the Legislature

Congress is the source of all federal law. The President cannot make law. The Supreme Court cannot make law. The vast federal bureaucracy cannot make law. Only the combined efforts

of the two branches of Congress—the House and the Senate—
can make law. No one and nothing else in our governmental
structure has any legislative power.

That means that the daily goings on of Congress are of central significance to Christians concerned about the State of the
Union.

As presently constituted, the House of Representatives has
435 members apportioned on the basis of population, and elected
every two years from among the fifty states. The Senate has one
hundred members, two from each state, elected to staggered six
year terms. Those five-hundred thirty-five magistrates have the
power to stop abortion, outlaw pornography, reverse deficit
spending, restrain educational repression, halt IRS tyranny,
transform criminal justice, and realign foreign affairs. If only
they would.

And they would if only Christians could bring the proper
kind of pressure to bear. For every road a proposed piece of legislation can take, there are innumerable options: road blocks
and detours, dead ends and short cuts, bottlenecks and thor-
oughfares. By knowing the lay of the land, by scouting out every
nook and cranny, by carefully surveying the map, Christians
can steer the House and Senate through humanism's obstacle
course out into the clear. After all, "the race is not to the swift,
nor the battle to the strong" (Ecclesiastes 9:11). For "wisdom is
better than strength" (Ecclesiastes 9:16).

If Christians are going to help restore America's greatness
they are going to have to learn the mechanics of Congress. They
are going to have to familiarize themselves with the legislative
process, and then involve themselves in that process.

There are several places to start: constituent education,
political action committees, and sub-committee hearings.

**By initiating constituent education programs Christians
can completely reshape the legislative agenda of Congress**.
Congressmen are elected as representatives of the people. They
are supposed to look out for their constituents' best interests.
They are supposed to support their concerns, advocate their
causes, and represent their views. Usually they don't though. It
doesn't really matter to them that they are out of line with the
folks back home because knowledge of their activities and voting

records rarely ever makes it out of the Washington area. They don't have to be accountable. Or at least they haven't had to be until now.

If Christians could develop an information network that let the constituents know what their congressmen were saying, how they were voting, and who they were allied with, two dramatic changes would instantly occur in the Legislature. First, a number of Congressmen would take this sudden notoriety and accountability to heart and vote responsibly for a change. And second, a number of Congressmen would be out on their heels come the next election.

It would not be terribly difficult for Christians to collect, print, and distribute the voting records of the five-hundred thirty-five members of the House and Senate. And with the high speed efficiency of *Contact America's* computer link-up and *C-Span's* televising of the various legislative sessions, gathering and disseminating such information is made all that much easier.

Congressional Report Cards, Candidate Score Cards, issue analysis reports, bill progression updates, and white paper documents ought to be a part of the routine vocabulary of the Christian. The humanistic juggernaut will continue to roll mercilessly over the land, crushing life and liberty as long as Christians turn a blind eye toward the irresponsible activities of Congress.

If a Christian presence is never felt through constituent education, if the Legislature is not called into account for their blatant advocacy of humanism, there is little hope that the walls of this nation can be rebuilt. Christians therefore need to learn the mechanics of congressional accountability. They need to bear fruit.

**By establishing a political action committee (PAC) Christians can shape not only elections but policy changes in the future.** Money talks. It can inflict great political pain or provide tremendous political rewards. Where letter writing campaigns, petition drives, and public protests have all failed, financial contributions have succeeded. A PAC is a campaign finance organization. Its primary purpose is to serve as a conduit of money. There is absolutely nothing wrong with the private financing of political campaigns. Unfortunately, over the past twenty-five years, the humanists have been doing the financing.

Most politicians realize by now that the evangelical Christian community is a vast untapped mine of money, manpower, and mailing lists. And they are out to exploit and exhaust that mine. Christian PAC's provide protection and direction for that mine. Instead of putting believers at the mercy of the humanistic political process, Christian PAC's obligate politicians to take the Biblical agenda more seriously. Knowing that a PAC has strict giving guidelines, clear priorities, and a positive agenda puts legislators on notice. It lets them know where their bread gets buttered, who pulls the strings, and how the game will be played. It creates an ecology of influence for Christians and provides assurance and insurance that ethics will enter the public policy debates in the future.

If a Christian presence is never felt through PAC financial designations, and if Congress is not obligated to see the force of morality in the market place, there is little hope that the walls of this nation can be rebuilt. Christians therefore need to learn the mechanics of political action committees. They need to bear fruit.

**By testifying before Congressional sub-committee hearings Christians can powerfully effect and affect the bottom end of the legislative process.** There are at least sixteen different stages that a bill must pass through before it is actually enacted as law. It must be introduced. It must be referred to committee. It must proceed through the appropriate sub-committees within that committee. It must then be subjected to hearings and mark-up. Next the bill must be reported to the full House. It is then put on the calendar. When the date for discussion on the floor finally comes up, consideration must be obtained. Then, consideration, discussion, and debate occurs. Next comes the voting stage. If the bill passes the House it is referred to the Senate where a similar, albeit shorter, consideration, committee, and floor process is followed. Once the Senate passes the bill, it goes before a joint committee of both branches to consolidate any differences. The completed bill then goes to the President for signing. Only then can the bill be published, classified, and codified as law. Anywhere along the way a bill can be altered, adjusted, or scrapped altogether, but the earlier strong support or opposition appears, the more influence that input will bring to bear.

That is why committee and sub-committee hearings are so crucial. Debate, discussion, and expert testimony in those early stages of a bill can decide whether it will be a strong moral and ethical piece of legislation or one more humanistic assault on truth and justice. Unfortunately, Christians have not taken advantage of the opportunities afforded by those hearings.

Where are the experts in law, medicine, family life, business, social welfare, science, and technology who can provide Congress with sound Scriptural answers to the nagging dilemmas of our time? Where are the Christian psychologists, sociologists, and geologists? Where are the Christian educators, economists, and journalists? Where are they, and why aren't they lending their expertise to the men and women who are formulating our laws?

Christians should contact their Congressmen, Senators, and the various evangelical lobbies, offering their services in the area of their discipline. They should contact the committee chairmen or the ranking minority leaders and have their names put into the hopper. Hundreds of hearings go begging for expert testimony every year. The opportunities for Christian witness are innumerable.

If a Christian presence is never felt at the committee or sub-committee level, if the only input during the formative stages of legislation is humanistic, there is little hope that the walls of this nation can be rebuilt. Christians therefore need to learn the mechanics of sub-committee hearings. They need to bear fruit.

Constituent education, political action committees, and sub-committee hearings — these are the keys to influencing the legislature. And influencing the legislature is the next major step toward restoring America's greatness.

### Influencing the Executive Branch

The President and his cabinet and staff have the awesome responsibility of enforcing the various laws enacted by the legislature. In recent years he has also become the primary source of vision, direction, and purpose for national and international policy making. Although he cannot *make* law, he can selectively emphasize law enforcement and judicial priorities. He also makes all the appointments to the federal bench.

Without a doubt the broad reach of his powers and influence make the President's office a critical concern for Christians. By virtue of his sweeping discretionary privileges, his executive order powers, his influence over the courts, and his access to the bureaucratic machinery, the President has the ability to cripple the onward march of humanism across the land. He could virtually end abortion on demand. He could almost instantly balance the budget. He could knock out the props of protectionism, welfarism, and socialism. He could, with the force of his office, put the legions of humanism out of places of power and prestige. If only he would.

And he would if only Christians could bring the proper kind of pressure to bear. The popularly elected President is especially sensitive to the pressures of public opinion. He depends on the good graces of the media for his political survival. He relies on special interests to keep him up to date and appraised on the issues. So why haven't Christians mounted strong public opinion campaigns to swamp the White House with outrage over the abortion holocaust? Why haven't Christians mobilized the media to call for strategic executive action against pornography? Why haven't Christians lobbied for a more sane economic policy, a more balanced educational policy, or a more realistic international policy?

If Christians are going to help restore America's greatness they are going to have to start doing these things. They are going to have to learn the mechanics of the Presidency. They are going to have to familiarize themselves with the executive process, and then involve themselves in that process.

There are several places to start: direct correspondence, utilization of the media, and professional lobbying.

**By corresponding directly with the White House, Christians can shape the President's opinions, preferences, and policies.** Only one out of every twenty Americans has *ever* written the President. Only one out of every two hundred has written more than once. And only one out of every ten-thousand has written more than five times. So while the mail room at the White House may receive several thousand pieces of correspondence every day only a few hundred address specific policy issues. And of those, only a tiny sampling fall into coherent categories. Because the President's staff tabulates these letters and then surveys them in the manner of a poll, any one letter can have a tremendous impact on the policy making process. Utilizing the letters as a guide to public opinion, the President may alter his views on an issue on the basis of just a few hundred letters and cards.

But not only does the White House keep tabs on public opinion indicators in its own mail, it watches those indicators in newspapers: letters to the editor, op-ed articles, and surveys. Thus, a letter to the local newspaper can multiply a Christian's influence significantly. After all, the pen is mightier than the sword.

The one thing that Plato and Marx, Thucidides and Newton, Calvin and Darwin, Locke and Hobbes, Luther and Rousseau, Augustine and Hegel all had in common was that they shook the world with a mere stroke of the pen. They all demonstrated that the art of correspondence is a powerful tool in the hands of zealous and passionate believers.

That is why it is so important for Christians to use proper mechanical skills when they write.

They should take great care in the composition and structure of their letters. In the White House mail room, as well as in the editorial office at the local newspaper, opinions usually receive consideration proportionate to the personal attention given to them. Pre-printed postcards and form letters simply won't receive much attention. A personal, neat, well-thought-out letter shows the staffer that the Christian correspondent really cares about the issue.

It is equally important for letters to be precise and concise. They should *briefly* outline how and why a particular bill or proposal or issue would adversely affect the individual, his family, his Church, his job, and/or his community. If a long detailed letter is felt to be really necessary, the primary concerns should be consolidated and summarized in the first paragraph or so — that may be all that will be read.

Obviously, the letter should be polite and respectful, but without compromising the issues. Concerns should be identified tactfully but straightforwardly, with a request for specific action. The letter should be encouraging, not abrasive. Like everyone else, magistrates, editors, and their staffs are likely to be polarized by demanding or threatening letters, but may become amenable to the Gospel as a result of a polite and uplifting note.

Correspondence really matters. It makes a difference.

If a Christian presence is never felt in the White House, if the humanists are the only ones with access to the Oval Office, there is little hope that the walls of this nation can be rebuilt. Christians therefore need to learn the mechanics of correspondence. They need to bear fruit.

**By utilizing the media to their best advantage Christians can develop a powerful platform for the truth**. The office of the President and the media have a love-hate relationship. They both depend on one another, need one another, and live off one another.

A comprehensive system of news releases, news contacts, media spokesmen, data retrieval, source procurement, public relations campaigns, expert analysis, and interview leads has been developed and craftily implemented by many of the most insidious humanistic groups: Planned Parenthood, the National Organization for Women, SIECUS, and the National Education Association. They have been able to nurture stories, do lead-generation, time breaking events, create desirable publicity, and shape public opinion. And all that goes a long, long way toward maintaining a high and influential profile at the White House.

So why have Christians failed to develop that kind of media acumen? Why have Christian organizations not been able to exploit the media as a wedge against the White House the way that the enemies of the faith have? The opportunities are there. The technology is there. The resources are there. All that is lacking is commitment for the long haul and the mechanical know-how to make it happen.

Christians need to support and to utilize existing media networks like *Contact America, Point of View,* and *Good News Communications.* They need to pray for and prepare for new opportunities to break in to ABC, CBS, NBC, CNN, PBS, and the BBC. On a local level they need to put together press packets, hold seminars on how to deal with the press, and develop long and short range strategies.

All this ultimately impacts the influence Christians will have with governmental officials, especially those in the executive branch.

If a Christian presence is never felt in the media, if the White House is never challenged with an alternative perspective in the press, there is little hope that the walls of this nation can be rebuilt. Christians therefore need to learn the mechanics of media utilization. They need to bear fruit.

**By sponsoring a lobbying presence in Washington Christians can begin to shape the perspectives of executive branch officials.** There are presently dozens of evangelical Christian organizations that maintain offices on Capitol Hill. Unfortunately, most of those offices serve little more purpose than being the locus of a fund raising machine. They are not actively involved in developing ongoing discipling relationships with the men and women in government. They are not actively producing alternative policy proposals for White House officials to consider. They are not even actively building action networks for the implementation of Biblical aims.

The humanists are certainly not sitting idly by. They have developed extensive lobbying campaigns focusing on virtually every perversion imaginable: They have instigated incest lobbies, pedophilia lobbies, abortion lobbies, pornography lobbies, etc., etc., ad nauseam.

Once again, Christians are being forced to play the game of catch-up.

One way to play that game and catch-up in a hurry is to lobby electronically. There is no replacement for a viable Washington presence, but when that is just not possible, computer wizardry is the next best thing.

The master of computer lobbying is Richard Viguerie. In 1964 he began developing a list of donors during Barry Goldwater's ill-fated presidential campaign. Viguerie recognized something early on: Goldwater had generated more *small* donations than any other presidential candidate in modern times. There were a lot of "true believers" out there on the grassroots level.

With the names of those "true believers" he was able to make a technological end run for a number of Christian causes. He was in fact credited with helping reorient the shape of government in Washington following the disastrous Carter Administration.

There were limits to Viguerie's lists, however. The biggest problem was their size. Because over the years he had collected so many names, small campaigns could not afford to use his services.

So, two of Viguerie's former employees, Larry Pratt, a Washington lobbyist, and computer whiz Frank Slinkman spent two years designing and redesigning a lobbying program to meet the needs of small and/or local Christian efforts. They originally designed the program for the TRS-80 Model I, but soon upgraded it for the Model III and the IBM-PC. They called the program POLSYS.

Each POLSYS disk can store more than 1000 names, and under each name there are a staggering number of "user-defined variables."

The system is quick, flexible, inexpensive, and powerful. It allows users to fire off letters to every key official on the White House Staff, key contacts in the media, and each of the members of the House, the Senate, and the judiciary in a matter of minutes.

This is the politics of the future. This is the kind of Christian cultural activism that can turn an issue around "spontaneously."

If a Christian presence is never felt in Washington, if the humanistic lobbies are never countered significantly, there is little hope that the walls of this nation can be rebuilt. Christians therefore need to learn the mechanics of lobbying. They need to bear fruit.

Direct correspondence, media utilization, and lobbying—these are the keys to influencing the Executive Branch. And influencing the Executive Branch is the next major step toward restoring America's greatness.

### Influencing the Judiciary

There was once a time when the courts were the greatest friends of Christendom in all of government.

In upholding the Northwest Ordinance of 1787, the Supreme Court asserted in 1791 that "Religion, morality, and knowledge, being necessary to good government and the happiness of mankind, schools and the means of righteous education should forever be encouraged."

In that same year the Court upheld the right of five ratifying states to protest the omission of a direct mention of God in the new Constitution saying, "Indeed the concern over the Christian status of the nation is well founded."

In 1825 the Court refused to hear complaints over a trade treaty between the U.S. and Russia that began with the words, "In the Name of the Most Holy and Indivisible Trinity." The Court simply rebuffed the criticisms, asserting that the treaty's preamble was "entirely legitimate."

In 1844 the Court argued in Vidol vs. Girard that "Christianity is part of our common law . . . its divine origin and truth are admitted and therefore it is not to be maliciously and openly reviled and blasphemed against, to the annoyance of believers or the injury of the public."

In 1892 the Court stated in Church of the Holy Trinity vs. U.S. that "No purpose of action against religion can be imputed to any legislation, state or national, because this is a religious people. This is historically true. From the discovery of this continent to the present hour, there is a single voice making this affirmation."

In 1930, in the case of U.S. vs. McIntosh, the Court said, "We are a Christian people, according to our motto. The right of religious freedom, demands acknowledgment, with reverence, the duty of obedience to the will of God."

In 1952, the Court argued in Zorack vs. Clauson that "We are a religious people whose institutions presuppose a Supreme Being."

Sadly, those days are now long gone. The Federal Courts and their adjunct courts all across the land have been transformed from being the friends of the faith into the enemies of the faith. Over the last thirty years school prayer has been banned, public access has been restricted, Christmas celebrations have been squelched, Christian schools have been harassed, and free speech has been denied. Under the guise of pluralism, the Courts have manipulated the tenuous doctrine of the "separation of Church and State" into a carte blanche for the humanistic proponents of an officially atheist state system.

If Christians are going to help restore America's greatness, they are going to have to find ways of reversing this dismal state of affairs. They are going to have to learn the mechanics of the judiciary. They are going to have to familiarize themselves with the judicial process, and then involve themselves in that process.

There are several places to start: jury nullification, aggressive litigation, and the testing of laws.

**By actively implementing the principle of jury nullification, Christians have a powerful influence over the courts.** The purpose of a jury is to put a check on the power of the magistrates by putting ultimate power in the hands of individual citizens. In a very real sense, the Founding Fathers gave each citizen three votes: the first was the free elections vote in order to choose their representatives, the second was the Grand Jury vote in order to prevent overzealous prosecutors from harassing the citizenry, and the third was the jury vote in order to restrain the courts from unjustly applying legitimate laws or from legitimately applying unjust laws. Thus the true function of the jury is to try not only the actions and the motives of the defendant, but the actions and the motives of the prosecution, the court, and the law as well.

According to the 1972 decision of U. S. vs. Dougherty, juries have the "unreviewable and irreversible power . . . to acquit in disregard of the instruction on the law given by the trial judge." In other words, the jury can ignore the prosecutor, ignore the judge, and even ignore the law if the courts and the law seem to be out of line with Biblical directives. This is the cherished doctrine of jury nullification that men like John Adams, James Madison, John Jay, and Alexander Hamilton struggled for so long.

Sadly, it is an almost forgotten doctrine. That is why it is so essential that Christians become informed jurors, to hold the courts in check. Thus, Christians need to *aspire* to jury duty, not *avoid* it. They need to apply themselves diligently so that they can be selected. They need to be certain never to disqualify themselves in pro-life cases or pornography cases or child abuse cases just because they hold moral convictions on those matters. Moral conviction is just *exactly* what the courts need right now.

If a Christian presence is never felt on trial juries, if only confirmed humanists sit and rule in our land, there is little hope that the walls of this nation can be rebuilt. Christians therefore need to learn the mechanics of jury nullification. They need to bear fruit.

**By aggressively pursing a program of litigation, Christians can set the judicial agenda over the next decade.** Why should the ACLU, Planned Parenthood, the NEA, NOW, and PAW be the only ones to take cases before the courts as a means of policy advocacy? Why should they be allowed to roam about the land like a hungry beast seeking those Christians whom they might devour? Why haven't Christians mounted both offensive and defensive measures to counter the humanists' well orchestrated assault on our legal system?

Although a few groups like the *Rutherford Institute* and the *Christian Legal Society* have begun to scratch the surface in these areas, much more needs to be done. Litigation needs to pour forth from the Christian community in torrents. Parents need to sue school districts over the debauched curriculum programs. Women abused by abortion need to sue the various media outlets for slander and deliberate misrepresentation of the facts. And Churches need to sue zoning commissions for discriminatory regulation. In the same way that the humanists have smothered believers over the last thirty years with their lawsuits, Christians need to take to the courts, fighting fire with fire. Christians need to stop waiting until they are sued to utilize the system to save the system.

If a Christian presence is never felt on the court dockets, if the legal supremacy of the humanists is not challenged, there is little hope that the walls of this nation can be rebuilt. Christians therefore need to learn the mechanics of aggressive litigation. They need to bear fruit.

**By creatively testing existing laws, Christians can force the courts to face up to their responsibility to administer justice.** The "defense of necessity" is a legal maneuver that argues that "lesser laws may be broken so that a greater good might be done." So for instance, breaking and entering a burning house to save a victim from the flames is not a crime. Likewise, assault and battery on a rapist in order to free his victim is not a criminal act. The "defense of necessity" may also be utilized to test laws that protect abortionists, pornographers, and child abusers. Sit-ins in clinics where the unborn are butchered in a wholesale slaughter are not simple cases of civil disobedience, but are opportunities to bring the "defense of necessity" into the courts, thereby testing the validity of the laws.

Humanists have been utilizing various legal tests to throw out Christian laws for years. Isn't it about time to turn the tables?

Christians need to find ways to test the laws that make it easy for the humanistic juggernaut to roll over the land. They need to risk the legal jeopardy necessary to strip away the protections that the abortionists, pornographers, and blasphemers now enjoy.

If a Christian presence is never felt in defense trials, if the only tests of law turn against the Gospel cause, there is little hope that the walls of this nation can be rebuilt. Christians therefore need to learn the mechanics of testing laws through the defense of necessity. They need to bear fruit.

Jury nullification, aggressive litigation, and the testing of laws — these are the keys to influencing the Judicial Branch. And influencing the judiciary is the next major step toward restoring America's greatness.

### Influencing the Bureaucracy

The bureaucracy is perhaps the most powerful "branch" of the American governmental system. It is certainly the largest and the most expensive. Yet it is nowhere mentioned in the Constitution. It was in no way envisioned by the Founding Fathers.

That makes for a very dangerous situation. Who monitors the bureaucracy? Who checks and balances its administration? Who even knows what it does?

When section 1008 of the Title X appropriations bill for population control went into effect, the bureaucratic minions simply ignored it and did whatever they jolly well pleased. Section 1008 stated that no funds could be issued to "any program or agency where abortion is utilized as a method of family planning." Despite that clear injunction, the Department of Health and Human Services has poured millions of dollars into the coffers of Planned Parenthood. In 1986 Title X subsidies to Planned Parenthood amounted to $42.5 million with another $97.2 million in Title XX allowances. Thus the bureaucracy illegally provided a full 62 percent of the budget for Planned Parenthood's program of murder, deception, and perversion, out of *our* tax dollars.

Similar stories of abuse could be told about IRS abuses, OMB excesses, EPA boondoggles, etc., etc.

Because the bureaucracy is unmonitored and unchecked, it is above the law. Quite literally. And run as it is by radical humanists, that means a real and substantial persecution of Christians and Christian causes.

Clearly, if Christians are going to help restore America's greatness they are going to have to learn the mechanics of the bureaucracy. They are going to have to familiarize themselves with the processes of bureaucratic administration, and then involve themselves in those processes.

There are several places to start: exposing anonymity, enforcing existing laws, and clogging the machinery.

**By exposing the anonymity of various individual bureaucrats, Christians can begin to bring the bureaucracy under control**. The great advantage of most civil servants over elected magistrates is the cover of anonymity. No one knows who they are. They are nameless and faceless. Thus, they are able to wield power and influence without fear of exposure or public reprisal. Often they can work for years behind the scenes, doing damage to life and liberty without any notoriety whatsoever. They are buried beneath a thick insulation of red tape, well disguised from the penetrating gaze of public and media.

But what if these well protected, long anonymous civil servants were exposed? What if they were held accountable for their actions? What if their names and faces and actions and activities were published for all to see? What if Christians began to put them under the same kind of scrutiny that elected officials must undergo?

Christians need to make the bureaucracy accountable for its policies and programs. They need to call individual administrators to task for their behind the scenes, godless activities. They need to do the research necessary to catalog the homes, file the addresses, computerize the lists, and monitor the decisions so that the civil servants can be made to *serve* the citizenry once again.

If a Christian presence is never felt in the individual lives of the bureaucrats, if their hidden humanism is left unexposed, there is little hope that the walls of this nation can be rebuilt. Christians therefore need to learn the mechanics of exposing the anonymity of the bureaucracy. They need to bear fruit.

**By calling for the enforcement of existing laws, Christians can greatly influence the bureaucratic agenda.** Every day, the bureaucracy publishes several hundred new pages of rules, regulations, statutes, policies, and restrictions that carry the force of law. But all too often these new ordinances in the *Federal Register* are contrary to existing law. They are nothing but an attempt to anonymously end run the legislature and the courts.

If Christians could monitor both the *Federal Register* and the policy programs that go unpublished, holding the various civil servants accountable to existing law, the humanistic loopholes would be virtually closed. Planned Parenthood would lose all its funding. The ACLU would lose its massive subsidies. And all the other anti-Christian programs would be thrown out into the cold. The administration of government would at long last be returned to the sanity of a standard of law.

This would mean that Christians would have to know the law. They would have to spring into action immediately when infractions occurred. And they would have to be willing to take the heat from a lot of very irate humanists.

If a Christian presence is never felt in the day to day operations of the bureaucracy, if existing laws are not upheld, then there is little hope that the walls of this nation can be rebuilt. Christians therefore need to learn the mechanics of enforcing existing laws in and around the bureaucratic framework. They need to bear fruit.

**By clogging the machinery of the bureaucracy, Christians can not only buy time for more permanent measures, they can reshape the way government operates.** The bureaucracy is a lumbering bumbling monolith. It is a vast Goliath. A monstrous giant. But a few Christians properly prepared can walk in David's footsteps and become giant killers. The bureaucracy has a full arsenal of howitzers. But howitzers are helpless against a swarm of mosquitoes.

When the humanistic cohorts in the bureaucracy begin to lay

waste to justice, mercy, and liberty, Christians need to swarm into the fray slowing, stalling, deterring, frustrating, distracting, and annoying. With speed, flexibility, and commitment a few insignificant mosquito-like maneuvers can clog the bureaucratic machinery for months. Ask for an official inquiry. Demand all the files on a given subject for the last decade under the Freedom of Information Act. Make phone calls. Write letters. Ask questions. Visit offices. Talk to supervisors. Make appeals.

If just a few Christians will run the gamut on the bureaucracy, the civil service could be frozen out of harm's way for months. Computerized information services like the efficient but inexpensive *American Press International* link-up or the *Contact America Network* can provide the information necessary to target particular offices, programs, or administrations. From there all it takes is a little time, a little effort, and a little creativity.

If a Christian presence is never felt in stalling the onward march of bureaucratic humanism, if the giant is not distracted by the mosquitoes, then there is little hope that the walls of this nation can be rebuilt. Christians therefore need to learn the mechanics of clogging the bureaucratic system. They need to bear fruit.

Exposing anonymity, enforcing existing laws, and clogging the machinery — these are the keys to influencing the bureaucracy. And influencing the bureaucracy is the next major step toward restoring America's greatness.

Bearing fruit obviously is no easy matter. Cultural change comes torturously slow and with great difficulty. There is no magic wand.

But it *can* be done.

## Word of Caution

This is all very dangerous stuff. It threatens the security of the status quo. It undermines the humanistic establishment's authority.

The enemies of God won't tolerate Christian cultural and political action.

There simply isn't enough room in their pluralism for faithful followers of the Lord Jesus Christ.

So, they have taken great pains to limit and inhibit Christian

activity in the society at large. Various IRS regulations, Federal
Election Commission regulations, and Federal statutes constrain
Christians, and especially ministers and Church congregations
from engaging in particular political actions.

If a Church is registered with the government as a 501(c)(3)
organization, the minister and the membership must pay close
attention to the details of these restrictions. Not all of them are
fair, or just, or right, but they do exist, and Churches should at
the very least know what the boundaries and risks are.

According to the IRS and the FEC, a Church or minister
"may not directly or indirectly participate in, intervene in (including the publishing or distributing of statements) any political campaign on behalf of or in opposition to any candidate for
public office."

Even so, the regulations do have loopholes.

For instance, the courts have ruled that a minister may allow
his name to be used in political ads in support of particular *issues*.
He may be identified in the ad as the minister of a particular
Church. He may even work with other individuals to establish a
PAC, though that committee must operate and "be viewed" as
separate from the Church. He may also engage in lobbying activities, circulate petitions, conduct voter registration drives,
loan mailing lists, and introduce candidates at services. And of
course, the courts have ruled that he may speak from the pulpit
to encourage the members of the congregation to become active
in every aspect of the political process. He may preach on the
importance of political activism and may pray for elected officials as often as he chooses. He may even lead public prayers for
the election of candidates who support a particular philosophy or
cause as long as the prayer "cannot be construed as a direct en-
dorsement of a candidate or candidates."

Recent rulings have placed limits on the time, the money, and
the manpower that can be poured into these activities. And, not
surprisingly, the IRS has made attempts to extend the restrictions
to non-registered Churches as well as to 501(c)(3) organizations.

Clearly, Christian cultural action will not be a cakewalk. The
humanistic establishment is bound and determined to eliminate
any and all risk-free options.

Welcome to the lions den!

## Conclusion

There is nothing more frustrating than working hard and committing time, energy, money, and manpower into a cause, but still seeing little or no return for the effort. Dr. Steven Hovda can tell you that. In order to keep a movement of Christian cultural change alive, the foundations of intercession, information, involvement, investment, and implementation must be fertilized with practical mechanical acumen so that a series of victories can be harvested.

It is essential therefore that Christians develop specific skills. They need skills to help them influence local government. They need skills to help them influence the Legislative Branch. They need skills to help them influence the Executive Branch, the Judicial Branch, and the Bureaucracy. They need political skills, administrative skills, entrepreneurial skills, legal skills, communications skills, and organizational skills. They need to have the kind of practical hands-on experience that will enable them to actually bear real fruit.

With an arsenal of new strategies, tactics, and agendas, Dr. Steven Hovda was ready to vivify his intercession, information, involvement, investment, and implementation plan. He was ready to claim a victory. He was ready to bear fruit.

"Our City Council passed an ordinance," he said, "that provided special protection and privileges to the homosexual community. It was put-up-or-shut-up time for us. We knew it. And they knew it. So we went to work."

Utilizing public forums, referendum electioneering, lobbying, judicial pressure, and a few technological end runs, Hovda and his small group of dedicated Christians were able to beat the humanists at their own game. The ordinance was overturned, overwhelmingly.

"Ah, the sweet, sweet savor of victory," he said, as he happily reminisced. "There is just nothing quite like it. And to know that it comes for the sake of the Kingdom makes it all that much more satisfying. For the first time we really did all our homework, and now look! We've *already* begun to bear fruit."

# WHERE THE RUBBER MEETS THE ROAD

As she listened to the presentation, her mind was buffeted back and forth between giddy excitement and complete frustration. She was tossed to and fro on the waves of doubt.

"I really agreed wholeheartedly with everything the speaker said," she confided later. "It was all the stuff that he *left out* that bothered me."

Nikki Lapscombe had attended a weekend workshop on Christian involvement in society. She had been exhorted to get involved in local affairs. She had been coaxed to sign petitions, subscribe to newsletters, and to host a home forum. She had been persuaded of the necessity to lay foundations of intercession, information, involvement, investment, and implementation. She had even been convinced that it was essential for her to begin to bear some fruit in the political realm by influencing local magistrates, national legislators, members of the executive branch, the judiciary, and the bureaucracy.

"I believed all that," she said. "I agreed with every bit of it. But I had this strong feeling that, somehow, that whole perspective was incomplete. Glaringly incomplete."

For several weeks Nikki wrestled with her concerns. Every time she opened the newspaper the necessity for Christian involvement in the world hit her right smack in the face. When she tucked her four small children into bed each night a sense of urgency tugged belligerently at her heartstrings. As she snuggled up next to her husband on the big overstuffed sofa, sipping hot tea and gazing into a crackling fire, her conscience nagged at their easy-may-care security. She slept fitfully knowing that the blessings she had come to know were in very real jeopardy as the humanistic juggernaut was even then ravaging the land.

"But I had come to believe that the answer to America's problems were not simply political," she asserted. "As I looked around at shattered families, broken relationships, corrupted schools, and scandalized Churches, I knew that in order to turn our country around we'd have to focus on more than just politics. Not that we should exclude politics. It's just that we need to think in broader terms than just that. We've got to make sure we don't turn Christianity into a political cult."

### Personalism and the Separation of Powers

The "separation of powers" doctrine is a cherished Constitutional concept whereby each of the *separate* branches of the government maintains *separate* institutions, *separate* jurisdictions, *separate* authorities, and *separate* functions. This kind of separation allows for another hallowed Constitutional concept—the "checks and balances" doctrine. Theoretically, the judicial, legislative, and executive branches are to restrain one another from inordinate influence or even tyranny. The Founding Fathers saw the separation of powers—and its corollary checks and balances—as essential doctrines for the fledgling American Republic to adhere to.

But they were not original ideas. The idea to separate powers and to institute checks and balances didn't suddenly dawn on Madison, Hamilton, Adams, Jay, and Hancock. It wasn't even unique to those men's mentors: Rutherford, Cromwell, Smith, and Locke. In fact, the doctrines come straight out of the Bible.

But, interestingly, the idea of distinct jurisdictions and balanced institutions is not limited in the Bible simply and solely to the area of civil government.

According to the Bible, the family and the Church are divinely established institutions right alongside the state. Each of them has its own jurisdiction, its own authority, and its own function. Each of them is a *separate* power. And each of them is to check and balance the others.

So, separation of powers and checks and balances are not simply functions of State action. Instead, they are to be carried out against the state by the family and the Church and vice versa. To center all the cultural power and activity around politics and the state is nothing more than statism. Even those conservatives who spend all their time and energy trying to *limit* the size and influence of the state are statist because their whole worldview is centered in the political realm. They are statists struggling for a small limited state, while the liberals are statists struggling for a large universal state. But they are both statist. The fact is that *all humanists* are ultimately statists, because they have nowhere else to turn to establish order and harmony than the state.

When Christians begin to believe that all, or even most, of America's ills can be cured by more state action, or less state action, or better state action, they, too, become statists. They turn Christianity into just what Nikki Lapscombe feared most: a political cult.

The Biblical perspective of social transformation is *personal*. It includes politics. It includes laying foundations of intercession, information, involvement, investment, and implementation. It includes influencing local government, legislators, the executive branch, the judiciary, and the bureaucracy. It includes all those things, but it includes a whole lot more. It includes reconstructed relationships. It includes restored families. It includes revitalized education. It includes revived Churches. And it includes renewed service. It is not statist—centered in and around a single divine institution. It is personal—separated out among and balanced between *all three* divine institutions and the *people* that compose them.

If Christians are going to rebuild the walls of this culture, if they are going to help to restore America's greatness, they are going to have to become politically involved. But that must not be where their involvement ends. They must not become statists, turning Christianity into a political cult. Instead, their plan of involvement must be centered on *people*. Their plan must focus on reconstructing relationships, restoring families, revitalizing education, reviving Churches, and renewing service, *as well as* remolding politics.

"That's where the rubber really meets the road," Nikki Lapscombe said. "People—if we ever forget them, we'll never make any headway."

### Reconstructing Relationships
Any businessman can tell you that the best kind of advertising is word of mouth. It is regular folks telling their friends, neighbors, and peers about a particular product or service.

People can only be hyped so much and so far. Commercials, campaigns, programs, and strategies are innately limited.

*People* are influenced most by *people*. People they know. People they trust. People that have good reputations. People that they care about.

That is why when Jesus sent his disciples out to win the world and to transform society, He told them to get personally involved with people (Matthew 28:19-20). They were to start with the folks they knew (Acts 1:8). They were to nurture relationships (2 Timothy 2:2). They were to have spotless reputations (1 Timothy 3:2). They were to be above reproach (Titus 1:6). They were to be personable, loving, kind, gentle, and a joy to be around (Galatians 5:22).

The way the Christian wins his battles involves winsomeness as well as confrontation (1 Peter 3:1-2). After all, love covers a multitude of sins (1 Peter 4:8).

Often, Christians get so involved in the political struggle for life and liberty, that they forget about the pivotal role that reconstructed relationships can play in rebuilding the walls of this land. They neglect the centrality of reconstructed relationships in restoring America's greatness.

Here, then, is how they can remedy that critical omission: they can work hard at constructing solid reputations, deep and abiding friendships, and committed programs of discipleship.

**First, Christians need to work hard at constructing solid reputations**. The scandal-wracked Christian community is held in anything *but* high esteem by the citizenry at large. And it is not simply because a few highly placed TV evangelists have been exposed as frauds. The *entire* Christian community has succumbed to compromise and engaged in public sinfulness. Graft, greed, corruption, and materialism are *common* Christian vices. Christian divorce rates are skyrocketing. Christian gossip is epidemic. Christian philandering is profligate. The lives of believers are all-too-often indistinguishable from the lives of unbelievers. They are promiscuous, concupiscent, and lascivious. Is it any wonder that the humanists hold Christians in low regard? Is it any wonder that they question their motives? Is it any wonder that they shriek in horror and dismay any time believers begin to make headway in civic or cultural affairs? If this nation is to be turned around in any measure, Christians will have to right these wretched wrongs. They will have to regain and retain high and honorable reputations among their neighbors, friends, and peers.

**Second, Christians need to work hard at constructing deep and abiding friendships.** The Biblical art of interpersonal devotion is an almost lost art today. People have acquaintances. People have companions. People have common interests. People have professional contacts. But very few people have real friendships past the days of adolescence. The dearth of interpersonal intimacy is especially true among men. The trust, confidence, loyalty, honesty, integrity, transparency, dependency, and accountability that comes with true friendship is lost on them. As a result, they do not have the reserves of strength, boldness, certainty, and commonality necessary for protracted spiritual and cultural warfare. Christians are picked off by burnout, fanaticism, loneliness, or temptation simply because they have failed actively and passionately to nurture this vital aspect of their lives. They have attempted to live and work as "Lone Rangers." And that simply does not, cannot, and will not work. If this nation is to be turned around in any measure, Christians will have to right these wretched wrongs. They will have to inculcate and incubate Godly and intimate friendships.

**Third, Christians need to work hard at constructing committed programs of discipleship.** Disciples are made one person at a time. Mass production has its place in the communication of the Gospel—through crusades, revivals, radio, and TV—but nurturing overcoming faith and resilient maturity is an intensely individualized process. It takes time. It takes effort. And it takes personalized attention.

In this instant-everything world, Christians tend to neglect the one-on-one dynamic of discipleship. They tend to abandon the time-consuming model of apprenticeship, of accountability, of oversight, of shepherding, of individuality, and of responsibility that is inherent in the Scriptural program of discipleship. The fact is, most Christians are left to grow—or stagnate as is so often the case—all on their own. They are expected to figure out inductively what to do, how to act, what to change, and whom to associate with. They are snatched like brands from the flickering flames of perdition and then tossed aside to smolder and grow cold at the edge of the camp. Evangelism is all too typically a "love 'em and leave 'em" affair. Is that any way to substantively transform the world?

Is that any way to influence a culture? Is that any way to inculcate enthusiasm for the Biblical plan for restoration? Clearly, if this nation is to be turned around in any measure, Christians will have to right these wretched wrongs. They will have to institute and institutionalize personalized programs of discipleship.

Constructing solid reputations, deep and abiding friendships, and committed programs of discipleships — these are the ways that Christians can rebuild relationships and thus transform society.

That's where the rubber meets the road.

### Restoring Families

When families fail, the entire society is placed into jeopardy. When families succeed, the entire society benefits.

This is because God charges the family with the responsibility of being society's basic building block (Genesis 9:1-7). It is central to virtually every societal endeavor under God: from education to charity (Proverbs 22:6, 1 Timothy 5:8), from economics to spirituality (Deuteronomy 21:17, Ephesians 6:1-4), from the care of the aged to the subdividing of the culture (1 Timothy 5:3-13, Genesis 1:26-28).

It is the family that is charged with the responsibility of infusing children with the principles of God's Word (Deuteronomy 6:6-7).

It is the family that is charged with the responsibility of upbraiding, restraining, and rebuking unrighteous behavior (Proverbs 23:13-14).

And it is the family that is charged with the responsibility of balancing liberty with justice, freedom with responsibility, and license with restriction (Deuteronomy 11:18-21). Ultimately, it is the family that shapes the course of the Church (1 Timothy 3:4-5, 12) and even of the state (1 Samuel 8:1-22).

So, if the family is weak, unstable, insecure, debilitated, demoralized — as it is in our land today — the entire structure of civilization is gravely at risk.

Leadership is a function of happy, wholesome, righteous, active, loving, vibrant, and challenging homes, not of conservative political parties. Vision is a function of Godly homes, not of far-sighted campaign platforms. Character, stalwartness, courage, efficiency, incorruptibility, excellence, confidence, dynamism, and integrity—these are all functions of Christian homes, not of civil orientation programs. The fact is, moms and dads loving, teaching, and disciplining their kids offer America more hope than all the political machinations of the Religious Right *ever* could.

Yet, all too often, Christians get so involved in the political struggle for life and liberty that they forget about the pivotal role that restored families can play in rebuilding the walls of this land. They neglect the centrality of restored families in reviving America's greatness.

Here, then, is how they can remedy that critical omission: they can work hard at integrating spiritual nurture, financial responsibility, and quality time back into their own family lives.

**First, Christians need to work hard at integrating spiritual nurture into their families**. Parents are charged by God with the awesome and fearsome responsibility of raising their children up "in the nurture and admonition of the Lord" (Ephesians 6:4). That's not primarily the job of the preacher, the Sunday School teacher, the youth director, the summer camp counselor, the TV evangelist, or the Christian school educator. It is first and foremost the job of parents. It is *their* job to inculcate prayer habits in their children by actually praying with them. It is *their* job to establish Bible study disciplines in their children by actually studying with them. It is *their* job to nurture a commitment to Body life by actually fellowshiping with them. It is *their* job to confirm a respect for the throne of God by actually worshiping with them. It is *their* job. It cannot be delegated, relegated, or dispatched.

Sadly, Christian families in our day have desperately attempted to do just that. In the hustle and bustle of these frantic and frenzied times, such things as family devotion, family catechisms, family prayers, and family altars have become musty, dusty archaisms. Husbands and wives don't pray together. Brothers and sisters don't study the Scriptures together. Parents and kids don't worship together. And the results have been disastrous. If this nation is to be turned around in any measure, Christians will have to right these wretched wrongs. They will have to reorder their priorities. They will have to place spiritual nurture at the forefront of their families' agendas.

**Second, Christians need to work hard at integrating financial responsibility into their families.** Again, God has charged parents with an enormous series of responsibilities. They are to guard their children from the ravages of greed, materialism, graft, and corruption on the one hand and poverty, paucity, deprivation, and debt on the other. They are to teach their children — and model in their own lives — Godly stewardship through the use of basic Biblical strategies like budgeting (Luke 14,16), saving (Proverbs 6), setting goals (Proverbs 1), investment (Matthew 21), the eradication of debt (Romans 13:8), and, of course, the tithe (Malachi 3:8-12).

Sadly, all too often Christians rant and rave about the fiscal irresponsibility of Washington, about deficits, inflation, taxes, and waste while their own houses are in utter disarray. Living way beyond their means, enslaved by credit, and bound by material compromise, they presume to pull pet Bible verses out of their repertoire of overly-rehearsed pietisms to bludgeon high-rolling, high-spending humanists. What hypocrisies! No wonder so few of the men and women in places of prominence and power pay heed to the Christian cause. If this nation is to be turned around in any measure, Christians will have to right these wretched wrongs. They will have to get their own houses in order. They will have to begin to untangle the complex snarl of financial irresponsibilities in their families and then establish patterns of holy and consistent stewardship.

**Third, Christians need to work hard at spending quality time with their families.** Tragically, the modern careerist myth that you can spend *quality* time with your family without having to spend *quantity* time with them has been accepted in a wholesale fashion by Christians in our day. Quality time isn't something that can be conjured at will out of a void. It is the natural product of nurture, constancy, consistency, and familiarity. Quality time takes time! It is only as intimate personal relationships develop over long and protracted blocks of dedicated time that parents and children, brothers and sisters, and husbands and wives can become what God really intended: a *real* family.

God charges parents with the responsibility to teach their children proper standards of physical health through regular hygiene (Leviticus 15; Numbers 19; Deuteronomy 23), exercise (1 Corinthians 16:18-21; 3 John 2), nutrition (Leviticus 7:22; Deuteronomy 32:14-15), and rest (Exodus 20:8-10; Psalm 23; Hebrews 4). They are to nurture their children in Godly character through discipline, literacy, and learning (Deuteronomy 4:9, 6:6-8; 2 Timothy 4:13). They are to afford their children emotional stability, spiritual vitality, financial responsibility, physical sensibility, and mental reliability. And all these tasks take time. A lot of time. Quality time *and* quantity time.

Sadly, most Christians are entirely unwilling to take that time. They are entirely unwilling to fulfill those responsibilities. And yet they expect to change the world? They expect to rid our land of the blight of abortion, pornography, and injustice? They expect to revitalize American culture? There's just no way! If this nation is to be turned around in any measure, Christians will have to right these wretched wrongs. They will have to begin to invest themselves and their time in the life of their families.

Reestablishing Spiritual nurture, rebuilding financial responsibility, and restoring quality time — these are the ways that Christians can revitalize their families and thus transform society.

That's where the rubber really meets the road.

## Revitalizing Education

"If you want to lead," quipped Napoleon to his generals, "you'll have to read." And he was right. Those men and women God raises up to influence and reform society must be well-informed, well-educated, and well-read. Daniel was known for his great learning (Daniel 1:17), as was Solomon (Ecclesiastes 1:16-18), Jesus (Luke 2:46-47), and the Apostle Paul (Acts 26:24). Solomon accumulated a massive library and was an encyclopedic chronicler of human knowledge (1 Kings 4:32-34), and the Apostle Paul cherished his books and parchments, yearning for them even during his imprisonment (2 Timothy 4:13). The early Church Fathers were brilliant and literate men who hungered for learning like mustangs hunger for cool sweet bluegrass: Clement of Rome, Ignatius, Gregory of Nyssa, Chrysostom, and John of Damascus.

Contrast that with the awful state of affairs in the community of believers today. Immersed in a sea of mediocrity, American Christians have sunk to an unimaginably low level of literacy.

As many as twenty-three million adults in this country are functionally illiterate. An additional thirty-five million are alliterate — they can read a few basics with difficulty, but that is about all. SAT score comparisons reveal an unbroken decline from 1963 to the present. Average verbal scores have fallen over fifty points and mathematics scores have dropped nearly forty points. Among the one hundred fifty-eight member nations of the United Nations, the United States ranks forty-ninth in its literacy levels! And this despite one of the most extensive and expensive school systems the world has ever seen. Education is, in fact, the second largest industry in the nation, spending more than a quarter trillion dollars every year, with nearly three million teachers and administrators, and the largest union in the world. Despite that, more than forty-five percent of all the products of that system cannot even read the front page of the morning newspaper.

And it appears that the situation is even worse among Christians. Due to a heritage of anti-intellectualism and pietistic isolationism, illiteracy and alliteracy run rampant in the Church. Only about eleven percent of the community of faith ever even visits a bookstore or library. And only about half of those actually buy books. The others purchase cards, or music, or trinkets, or gifts. The hardback book trade is supported by a mere five percent of the Christians in this country.

Our ethnocentricity tends to make us think that our country at this time is the best-educated, most advanced, and most sophisticated society of all time. It tends to make us think that our Church, at this time, is the most literate, best informed, and most sound of all time. But nothing could be farther from the truth.

How are Christians supposed to turn this nation around if they don't know what's going on in the first place? How are they going to restore the foundations of grace, mercy, and truth to this culture if they have yet to study, analyze, critique, research, read through, compare, contrast, synthesize, and summarize the vast storehouse of wisdom at their disposal in books? How seriously should the humanists take the Gospel agenda if the majority of its adherents are basically dysfunctional and illiterate?

Often, Christians get so involved in the political struggle for life and liberty that they forget about the obvious. They forget about the pivotal role that revitalized education can play in rebuilding the walls of this land. They neglect the centrality of revitalized education in restoring America's greatness.

Here then is how they can remedy that critical omission: They can work hard to restore spiritual vitality, academic excellence, and functional practicality to the educational process.

**First, Christians need to restore spiritual vitality to the curriculums of their children.** Education is not simply a transfer of naked neutral facts to the ready receptacles of young minds. It is the communication of an entire worldview. Facts are meaningless until they are fitted into a grid of interpretation, until they are located on a map of reality. That is why the Bible describes education as a parent-directed process of discovery and discipleship, as opposed to a professionally-directed program of discipline and didactae (Deuteronomy 6:4-9). It is not simply designed to enable children to draw from a repertoire of historical or mathematical trivia on command. Instead, it is the sovereignly appointed means of passing on the legacy of the covenant from one generation to the next. "Readin', writin', and 'rithmetic" are, thus, just as clearly opportunities to communicate the grace of Jesus Christ as "Bible class" is.

There is no generally accepted term in our educational vocabulary for this kind of learning—the Germans call it *erziehung*, the Russians call it *raspitanie*, and the French call it *educatione*. The best English equivalents would be something like "upbringing," "character training," or "admonitive nurture," expressions that sound oddly irrelevant to the schooling process to us. They speak of values, morals, motives, ethics, and patterns of social response, and in our society we've actually tried to separate those things from the educational system. Of course, in so doing, the educational system has been crippled.

Sadly, Christians have not only gone right along with this scandalous laming of learning, they have led the parade of fools who march through time trumpeting folly and irrelevance. They have willfully chosen to ladle the dust of old, broken cisterns rather than to drink deeply from the cool, still waters. But, if this nation is to be turned around in any measure, Christians will have to right these wretched wrongs. They will have to begin to infuse the educational programs of their children with substantial moral and spiritual content.

**Second, Christians need to restore academic excellence to the curriculums of their children.** At the time our nation was founded, a basic liberal arts education included a comprehensive study of Greek, Hebrew, Latin, and the literary classics of Plato, Aristotle, Thucidides, Aristophanes, Josephus, Augustine, Aquinas, Luther, Calvin, Knox, Milton, Rutherford, Rousseau, Voltaire, and Locke. It included physics, astronomy, geography, history, civics, logic, philosophy, theology, biology, composition, grammar, oratory, architecture, music, literature, and navigation. And that was just a *basic* education. Even in the rough-and-tumble pioneer schools—where kids could only attend between harvests, where every age group crowded into one room, and where time, money, and resources were extremely limited—the curriculum put to shame our modern and sophisticated schools. It's not that under the threat of a hickory switch those schools could command a higher level of academic discipline. They actually created a *hunger* for learning. They stimulated in their students a desire to grow and learn. They were rooted in the idea that nothing less than the best is good enough for servants in the kingdom of the Lord Jesus.

Sadly, that holistic approach to glorifying God with our all in all has been lost in our day. Christians have, by and large, adopted the pagan philosophy of pragmatism, thinking that they'll do just enough to get by in this world, and no more. Especially where it comes to academics. When was the last time you heard a believer talk nonchalantly and inconspicuously about genuinely intellectual pursuits? Such things are scorned in the Church today. They are perceived as superfluous and prideful. But, if this nation is to be turned around in any measure, Christians will have to right these wretched wrongs. They will have to begin to give the educational programs of their children a stout transfusion of academic excellence. How else are they supposed to overcome the enemy?

**Third, Christians need to restore functional practicality to the curriculums of their children.** Life is rough in the big city. The cold, cruel world comes as quite a shock to most kids fresh out of high school or college. And, for most of them, the world is even colder and crueler than need be, simply because they were entirely unprepared for it. More than 76% of all high school graduates and an astonishing 62% of all college graduates have no readily transferable job skills. And we wonder why it seems like we have to start from scratch economically with each new generation!

The fact is that since we have abandoned the age-old systems of apprenticeship and indenturing, our kids are forced to enter the marketplace without the skills necessary to succeed. Education has become a combination of therapy and baby sitting. Instead of laying the foundations for a life of industry, productivity, service, and stewardship, our kids are just "doing time." They are just wasting time. They idle their days and weeks and years away. And then they walk out into the work-a-day world as lost as a goose in a hail storm. They have no trade. They have no vocation. They have no skills. They have no direction. They have no training. And they have no future.

Do we really believe that the youth of this nation are our hope? Do we really believe that if this nation is to be turned around in any measure, they will have to help us do it? If so, then Christians will have to right these wretched wrongs. They will have to begin to make the educational programs of their children more practical. They will have to prepare them for the marketplace, for the real world, and for the future.

Restoring Spiritual vitality, academic excellence, and functional practicality—these are the ways that Christians can revitalize education and, thus, transform society.

That's where the rubber really meets the road.

## Reviving Churches

The Church has become the spurned and neglected stepchild of the modern evangelical movement. She is perceived as being moss-backed and archaic, awkward and irrelevant. She is regarded as little more than a water-boy to the game of life.

Part of the reason for this horridly low estimation of the

Church is due to the fact that the Church has always limped through history. People look at the manifest weaknesses of Christ's Bride, assuming that her lame and crippled estate is justification for minimizing her import.

Actually, quite the opposite should be the case. The Church's limping through history is actually a *confirmation* of God's anointing. God told Satan just after the Fall that the Righteous Deliverer, Jesus Christ, would crush his head. But He also said that, in the process, the heel of the Lord would be bruised (Genesis 3:15). Thus, the limp of Christ's Body is a sign of victory, *not* a sign of defeat. So, for instance, when Jacob, the father of Israel's twelve tribes, wrestled through the night at Peniel, he limped ever after as a sign of God's approval (Genesis 32:31). Similarly, the Apostle Paul, father of the Gentile Church, was given a thorn in the flesh. Since thorns grow along the ground, that thorn was (at least symbolically) in his foot. It kept him limping in the eyes of men (2 Corinthians 12:7), and yet it was in this weakness that Christ's power was affirmed and perfected (2 Corinthians 12:9). When the Church limps through history, believers need not be frustrated or discouraged. On the contrary, they should be encouraged that God's Word is sure and true, and that her victory has, indeed, already been won. They should hold the Church in higher estimation than ever before.

The fact is, what the Church does and doesn't do directly affects the course of civilization. It determines the flow of historical events (Revelation 5-6). It is a hub around which the gusting, swirling winds of time turn.

It is the *Church* that has the keys to the Kingdom (Matthew 16:19). It is the *Church* that has the power to bind and to loose (Matthew 18:18). It is the *Church* that shall prevail over the gates of hell (Matthew 16:18). It is the *Church*—not para-Church groups, not evangelistic associations, not political action committees, not special interest groups, not ecumenical rallies, but the *Church*—that can catalyze the kind of social transformation necessary to turn this nation around.

Just imagine what kind of impact Christians could, and would, be able to have in this culture if only the Church would awaken from her deep slumber and move with righteous passion across the land! Imagine what would happen if the Church would actually pray with fervor, minister with mercy, act with conviction, preach with power, counsel with wisdom, teach with clarity, and serve with gladness! Imagine what would happen if the Church would actually take her Great Commission seriously and shine the bright light of the Gospel into the cavernous darkness of modern American culture! Why, *everything* would change. Our entire nation would be thrown into an upheaval of grace and holiness. From MTV to Washington, D.C., from the classroom to the courtroom, from the ball-park to the benchmark, everything would be vivified by the searing, cleansing flames of revival.

Often, Christians get so involved in the political struggle for life and liberty that they forget about the obvious. They forget about the pivotal role that revived Churches can play in rebuilding the walls of this land. They neglect the centrality of revived Churches in restoring America's greatness.

Here then is how they can remedy that critical omission: They can work hard to restore Body Life, effectual discipline, and genuine refreshment to the Church.

**First, Christians need to restore a fully functional Body Life to the Church**. Mutual ministry is the way the Church is supposed to operate. Because every member of the Church has been endowed with particular and peculiar Spiritual gifts (1 Peter 4:10), he or she must exercise those gifts in order for the Body to be all that God has intended (1 Corinthians 12:7). That is why the New Testament so heavily emphasizes the "one another" commands as the primary relational qualifiers in the Body. Because they are members of *one another* (Ephesians 4:25), Christians are to love *one another* (Romans 13:8), build up *one another* (1 Thessalonians 5:11), serve *one another* (Galatians 5:13), defer to *one another* (Philippians 2:3), admonish *one another* (Colossians 3:16), comfort *one another* (1 Corinthians 12:25), and encourage *one another* (1 Thessalonians 5:11). They are to spur *one another* on toward love and good deeds (Hebrews 10:24), always bearing with *one another* (Colossians 3:13), accepting *one another* (Romans 15:7), waiting on *one another* (1 Corinthians 11:33), and fellowshipping with *one another* (1 John 1:7). They are never to speak against (James 4:11), complain against (James 5:9), or judge *one another* (Romans 14:13). Instead, they are to be of the same mind

(Romans 12:16), being subject to (Ephesians 5:21), and having forbearance for *one another* (Ephesians 4:2). They are to bear *one another's* burdens (Galatians 6:2), living in peace with *one another* (1 Thessalonians 5:13), and confessing sins to *one another* (James 5:16). In short, Christians are commanded by God to give preference in their lives to *one another* (Romans 12:10). They are whole-heartedly to commit themselves to Body Life. When they actually do that, not only is the entire Church fit for the work of the ministry, but the entire culture falls under the sway of wave after wave of confident, zealous, and thoroughly equipped believers (Ephesians 4:12-13).

Sadly, Body Life has all too often been relegated by the modern evangelical Church to the realm of theory. Mutual ministry has been replaced by professional ministry. Spiritual gifts lie dormant and unused. The "one another" commands go unheard and unheeded. If this nation is to be turned around in any measure though, Christians will have to right these wretched wrongs. They will have to revive the Church by restoring a fully functional and fully orbed ministry of the people, by the people, and for the people.

**Second, Christians need to restore effectual discipline in the Church.** Blatant, flagrant, perpetual sin simply must not be harbored and sheltered by God's chosen people. If sin is casually tolerated, the Church is defiled (1 Corinthians 5:6-13), evangelism is stifled (1 Corinthians 5:1-5), and victory is denied (Joshua 7:1-15). The abundant grace and forgiveness of God is not an excuse for libertine and promiscuous acceptance of wicked behavior (Romans 6:1-2). On the contrary, the mercy of God calls us to a communion of holiness and purity (Romans 6:3-11). Every member of the Church fails and falls from time to time (Romans 3:10-23), but patterns of heinous sin cannot and must not enter their lives (1 Corinthians 6:9-11). And so, if those patterns do crop up, the Church is obligated to take disciplinary action (Matthew 18:15-20). The purpose of Church discipline is not punitive but restorative. It builds into the Body accountability, responsibility, and respectability. It erects a hedge of protection and a boundary of fear around the people of the covenant.

Sadly, this dimension of God's plan for the Church has been utterly and completely ignored by the modern evangelical

Church in America. It seems that what the Bible has to say about internal integrity is simply too harsh, too controversial, too difficult, and too combative for a Church hell bent on numerical ascendancy and pecuniary glory. And, as a result, sin and scandal run rampant through the evangelical community like Sherman's troops through Atlanta, laying waste to anything and everything in sight. Instead of rousing an unflinching and prophetic call for repentance and discipline, the Church stands idly by while the enemies of the Gospel make a mockery of Christ and His Kingdom. Clearly, if this nation is to be turned around in any measure, Christians will have to right these wretched wrongs. They will have to rekindle the fires of holiness and integrity by restoring accountability and discipline to the Church in our day.

**Third, Christians need to restore genuine Spiritual refreshment to the Church.** When God's people assemble themselves together, they are to lie down in green pastures beside still waters (Psalm 23:2). As they gather around the throne of grace, they are to take refuge and find sanctuary (Psalm 61:1-4). They are to enter His gates with thanksgiving and His courts with praise (Psalm 100:4). In other words, they are to find rest (Hebrews 4:1-13), restoration (Psalm 19:7), reconciliation (Psalm 32:3-6), and recompense (Psalm 73:15-24) when they worship. Yes, Church membership involves duty, responsibility, commitment, service, obedience, deference, and sacrifice. Yes, Christians should go to Church to learn, to share, to serve, to give, and to work. But, first and foremost, they are to relax in the joy of the Lord as they collectively recall and reiterate the divine order of redemption.

Sadly, the modern Church has lost sight of this important reality and, as a result, the people of God come away from worship no more refreshed, no more ready for the battles ahead, than when they went in. Ignoring sanctity, sanctuary, and sacrament, most evangelical Bodies turn to wild extremes: "lecture hall" worship, "entertainment hall" worship, or "existential encounter" worship. They ignore the rich legacy that Churchmen of the past have left them and rush headlong into modern diversions and distractions from Godly refreshment. The modern tendency to turn the Church into either an Ecclesiastical Disneyland or an Empirical Museum is a far cry from the Biblical ideal of a vibrant, dynamic, and vivifying wellspring of strength, hope, and gladness. There can be no question that if this nation is to be turned around in any measure, Christians will have to right these wretched wrongs. They will have to return to the sure and secure foundations of true worship, restoring genuine Spiritual refreshment to the Church in our day.

Restoring Body Life, effectual discipline, and genuine refreshment—these are the ways that Christians can revive the Church and, thus, transform society.

That's where the rubber really meets the road.

## Conclusion

Christianity has answers. It offers solutions to the nagging, plaguing problems of our day.

Some of the solutions Christianity offers a world blighted by poverty, injustice, disease, and calamity are overtly political.

But, only some.

Christianity is a fully orbed worldview, and so it includes politics in its broad purview. But, it also includes much, much more. Christianity is by no means a political cult.

In the plan to redeem the societies that God implanted in the Bible and entrusted to Christianity are innumerable other institutions, strategies, and agendas. If any one of them is slighted, then the efforts of Christians in the political arena are doomed to failure.

That is precisely the realization that Nikki Lapscombe was coming to as she struggled with the level of her involvement and commitment to social and cultural transformation.

That is precisely the realization that *all* Christians must come to if they are to rebuild the walls of this culture, if they are to help restore America's greatness.

*Every area of life* must be yielded to the Lordship of Jesus Christ. Politics and personal relationships. Families and Churches. Institutions and communities. Now that's where the rubber *really* meets the road.

# PART FOUR

## THE AGENDA

After all is said and done, more is said than done.

Mark Twain

T E N

# SETTING THE PACE

It was a grisly scene.

The two men stared out in disbelief at the carnage that lay before them. Scattered throughout the rubbish heap were the twisted, broken bodies of several dozen children. A severed arm here. A mangled leg there. A contorted torso. A pair of crushed skulls. Anguished unseeing eyes in faces bathed in blood. Nauseating mutilation amidst the garbage of discarded coke cans, emptied ashtrays, fast-food wrappers, and other assorted office litter.

Robert Rudd, a bank vice-president, and Kevin Lambert, a student, gasped for their breath, their emotions tearing at their minds and their bodies. They had stumbled upon the scene of this awful awesome crime quite by accident. And they were entirely unprepared for what they saw there. Obviously.

"Until that moment," Lambert would later say, "abortion was almost a theoretical thing for me. I was vehemently against it. I was actively involved in various pro-life activities. My wife worked in a ministry to women in crisis pregnancies. I prayed. I picketed. I did all those things that I felt like the Bible had commanded Christians to do. But it was still kind of abstract. It was statistics, numbers, trends, ideologies, and dogmas. It wasn't really people. It wasn't really *children*. Not until we saw them."

"When we walked back behind Planned Parenthood's building," added Rudd, "we were already morally and intellectually committed to seeing that this horrible holocaust come to a complete halt in this nation. We were already convinced that the multi-million dollar abortion industry was an abomination to God and a disgrace to man. What the sight of those butchered children did for us was to change our sense of purpose, our perspective of time."

"Of course, it angered us," said Lambert. "It impassioned us. It frightened us. It overwhelmed us. But more than anything, it enabled us to see time in a whole new light."

"It showed us quite clearly, for perhaps the first time," said Rudd, "that time is actually an *ethical* issue."

## Time

According to the Bible, time is indeed an ethical issue. The Greeks thought of time as an impersonal cyclical force. The Romans believed that time was a neutral tool of measurement. And the Persians held that time was an illusion to be ignored. But God made it clear to the Hebrews and early Christians that time was an integral aspect of His moral program. He revealed to them the essential part that time plays in the work of redemption.

Though God exists outside the constraints of time, He does not attempt to evade or usurp it. He works in and through time. From the very beginning, when He established time in the warp and woof of creation, to the very end, when He will confirm time in the infiniteness and glory of eternity, God wove the essence of time into every aspect of reality (Genesis 1:5; Revelation 20:4).

This inescapable Biblical emphasis on linear chronology gave God's covenant people a distinctive awareness of their place and purpose in history. Their peculiarly forward-looking, dynamic sense of time was in stark contrast with the static and conservative Greeks, Romans, and Persians. It gave them a sense of destiny. It enabled them to inculcate a strong commitment to development, change, and progress. It enabled them to give impetus to multi-generational programs of social transformation. It enabled them to undertake the construction of great cathedrals, the exploration of uncharted seas, and the investigation of scientific wonders. It provided them with a work ethic, a sense of stewardship, and a commitment to their progeny.

This compelling and culture-changing conception of time suffuses past (1 Corinthians 10:6), present (Mark 1:15), and future (John 16:25) with purpose, and significance. It gives meaning to such diverse activities as domestic responsibilities and work (Genesis 29:7; Isaiah 28:24-25), travelling and residing (Deuteronomy 2:14), feasting and fasting (Judges 14:12; Psalm 37:19), toiling and resting (John 9:4), beautifying and embalming (Esther 2:12; Genesis 50:3). It lends appropriateness, and indeed *sanctity* to the basic rites of passage: birth (Ecclesiastes 7:1), youth (Ezekiel 16:22), menstruation (Leviticus 15:25), marriage (1 Samuel 18:19), childbearing (Psalm 127:3), maturity (Psalm 1:3), old age (Job 5:26), and even death (Genesis 50:4). For in the sovereign will of God there is "a time for every purpose under heaven" (Ecclesiastes 3:1). There are times of temptation (Luke 8:13), refreshment (Acts 3:19), distress (Nehemiah 1:7), appeal (Psalm 50:15), disgrace (2 Kings 19:3), vengeance (Isaiah 61:2), rebuke (Isaiah 13:13), rest (Jeremiah 27:22), affliction (Lamentations 1:7), cleansing (Ezekiel 36:33), destruction (Jeremiah 47:4), wrath (Isaiah 13:13), and salvation (Isaiah 49:8).

> To everything there is a season, a time for every purpose under heaven: a time to be born, and a time to die; a time to plant, and a time to pluck what is planted; a time to kill, and a time to heal; a time to break down, and a time to build up; a time to weep, and a time to laugh; a time to mourn, and a time to dance; a time to cast away stones, and a time to gather stones; a time to embrace, and a time to refrain from embracing; a time to gain, and a time to lose; a time to keep and a time to throw away; a time to tear, and a time to sew; a time to keep silence, and a time to speak; a time to love, and a time to hate; a time to war, and a time to peace (Ecclesiastes 3:1-8).

According to the Biblical scheme of things, there is nothing impersonal about time or history, or all those events that fill up time and history. They are all imbued with the grace and mercy of God's immutable purpose.

In practical terms, the Biblical notion of time drives God's covenant people with a passionate *urgency* while simultaneously soothing them with a calm *patience*.

It was a reorientation to this coexistent urgency and patience that Rudd and Lambert experienced after witnessing Planned Parenthood's handiwork. It was a reorientation to the Biblical perspective of time.

If Christians are going to rebuild the walls of this land, if they are going to help restore America's greatness, they are going to have to be similarly reoriented. They are going to have to set their clocks and plan their schedules according to God's urgent, yet patient, agenda.

## Urgency

Life is short. Needs are great. And imperatives are strong. All this makes for urgency.

Virtually every Biblical injunction about the use of time underlines the importance of *each moment that passes*. It is an ethical imperative to act and act quickly when lives are at stake, when justice is on the line, when truth is in jeopardy, when mercy is at risk, when souls are endangered, and when the Gospel is assaulted.

Christians are adamantly admonished to "make the most of the time" (Ephesians 5:15). They are to "redeem the time" (Colossians 4:5). And they are to utilize "every day to the utmost" (Hebrews 3:13). There is no room for procrastination or contemplation in these times of trouble, distress, and calamity. Christians must seize the day. Decisiveness, determination, singlemindedness, constancy, diligence, and passion must inform their agenda as they face off against the minions of inhuman humanism.

The pace they set should be fervent. For the task before them is urgent. It will not easily be dispatched.

## Patience

Victory will not be won in a day, however fervently Christians act. It will take time, perhaps generations.

In the interim, Christians are to be confident that God's sovereignty holds the times and the seasons in His hands. They are under His control.

Though times are hard and all the earth cries out under the burden of wickedness, injustice, and perversion, Christians can rest in the assurance that God is playing the keys of providence according to the score of His own devising. They need not be anxious (Philippians 4:6). They need not worry (Matthew 6:25). They need not fret (Luke 12:22).

Such a perspective on time is the attribute of Holy patience.

Patience is a fruit of the Spirit (Galatians 5:22). It is an attribute of love (1 Corinthians 13:4). And it is a qualification for leadership (2 Timothy 2:24).

In times of persecution (1 Peter 2:20), suffering (James 5:10), and confrontation (1 Thessalonians 5:14), patience is to be the Christian's over-riding concern. As he draws into battle against humanism's forces of darkness he is to be calm, confident, and collected.

The pace he sets should be steady. For the task before him will not soon be dispatched.

### Both-And

The Scriptural perspective of time impels Christians to work for reform in culture with *both* urgency *and* patience. Unlike the Greeks, Romans, and Persians, they are not forced to choose either-or.

But how are they to forge such a balance in their lives? How are they to fashion their agendas so that they match God's agenda?

Very simply, they must *sanctify* the time.

No Christian's time is his own. It is not his to dispose of as he chooses. He has "been bought with a price" (1 Corinthians 6:20), therefore he is to set his days, weeks, and years apart to the Lord for His glory (Romans 14:6-12).

In the Old Testament, *the days* were divided into eight periods: dawn, morning, midday, dark, evening, and three night watches. These were distinguished by times and seasons of prayer (Psalm 55:17; Daniel 6:10). In the New Testament, the value of this kind of "liturgical clock" is affirmed by the early disciples who punctuated their urgent task of evangelization with the patient discipleship of regular Spiritual refreshment (Acts 3:1).

Similarly, *the weeks* of God's people are ordered with purpose and balance. Centered in the Old Testament around Sabbath sacrifices, and in the New Testament around the Lord's Day sacraments, the weeks established Biblical priorities for the people by giving form to function and function to form (Deuteronomy 5:12; Hebrews 10:24-25). The "liturgical calendar" enabled them to wait on the Lord and thus to "run and not be weary" and to "walk and not be faint" (Isaiah 40:31).

And finally, even *the years* were given special structure and significance to reinforce the Biblical conception of time. In ancient Israel, feasts, fasts, and festivals paced the believers' progression through the months (Exodus 13:6-10; Psalm 31:15). The early Church continued this stewardship of time, punctuating years with the "liturgical seasons": Advent, Christmas, Epiphany, Lent, Easter, Ascension, and Pentecost. Thus, God's people were enabled and equipped to run the race (Philippians 2:16), to fight the fight (Ephesians 6:10-18), to finish the course (2 Timothy 4:7), and to keep the faith (2 Timothy 3:10).

At every turn, day in and day out, week in and week out, year in and year out, God's covenant people were to find ways to reinforce the practical balance between urgency and patience. They were to disciple and discipline their clocks, calendars, and seasons to be diligent, passionate, and active yet all the while resting assured in God's ultimate and sovereign control. They were to set their time apart to the Lord for His glory. They were, in other words, to reorient themselves to the Biblical perspective of time.

### Craftsmen of Time

Throughout the history of the Church there have been innumerable sterling examples of Godly men and women who actually did that. They were able to balance urgency and patience so that they accomplished much for the glory of God without hectically jeopardizing their health, their sanity, or their faith.

**Hilary of Poitiers (315-367), carefully crafted his perspective of time to fit the Biblical agenda.** He turned his small Church in rural Southern France into a remarkable hive of activity. He was not only a conscientious pastor, he was an educator, a musician, a composer, an author, a theologian, a social activist, and an artist. He was constantly at work on a new project: opposing Arianism with unswerving vigor, devising new methods of teaching Christian doctrine through metrical hymns, or writing exhaustive exegetical commentaries on Scripture portions. One of his adversaries once said that Hilary could not be defeated "for he seems to have more hours in a day, to accomplish more tasks than any other man alive." There was no question that he comprehended the essential urgency of redeeming the time and making the most of every opportunity. Yet he was not a harried man. He ordered his days, weeks, and years with the kind of patience and confidence that can only come to men reconciled to God's sovereignty. He found the Biblical balance between urgency and patience, and, thus, he was used mightily of God to change his family, his Church, and his community for Christ.

**Sava of Trnova (1175-1235), carefully crafted his perspective of time to fit the Biblical agenda.** The third son of Serbia's King Stephen I, Sava slipped out of the royal palace at the age of sixteen and secretly became a monk on Mt. Athos. Four years later he was joined there by his father, who had abdicated from the throne. Together they founded a retreat center for Serbian Christians, which exists even to this day, as one of the seventeen "ruling houses" on Athos. There they disciplined their days, weeks, and years according to God's agenda, and taught hundreds of others how to do the same thing in their own lives. In 1208, Sava left the serenity of the retreat and returned to Serbia, where the rivalry of his brothers had led to anarchy. He established a missionary work at Studenitsa, along the Yugoslav Coast, and from there set about the urgent task of reordering the chaos of the land with all due diligence and verve. He reorganized the Church, consolidated the throne, encouraged commerce, reopened trade, sponsored the arts, and enforced justice. He was constantly on the go, everywhere at once: working, encouraging, teaching, guiding, writing, and judging. Yet he always took time out to rest and rely on God's provident provision. From time to time he would retire from the pressures of his fervent activity to an inaccessible hermitage near Studenitsa to gain strength for perseverance in the urgent tasks before him. Clearly, he too found the Biblical balance between urgency and patience, and thus he was used mightily of God to change his family, his Church, and his community for Christ.

**John Knox (1513-1572), carefully crafted his perspective on time to fit the Biblical agenda.** Scotland's restless activist was a fiery preacher of the doctrines of grace who fell in and out of favor with the rulers of the land so many times that he had a permanent house in Geneva for use during his frequent exiles. When at home in Scotland, he was a tireless worker: writing, organizing, translating, planning, and preaching. When in exile, his schedule was no less fervent: pastoring the other exiles, pamphleteering, negotiating, and preaching. When civil war broke out at home in 1559, he rushed into the fray. By the summer of

1560, his band of followers controlled Edinburgh and were over-seeing an extraordinary revival that had an international im-pact. Through it all, however, Knox found time to take refresh-ment from the deep cool pools of God's providence. During one of his frustrating exiles in Geneva he wrote, "Our Sovereign's Superintendence of the course of human events is sure solace provoking patience amidst crisis, surety amidst urgency." He ordered his days, weeks, and years according to God's agenda, content to do his part with all diligence, but then leaving the rest to God Almighty. So, he too found the Biblical balance between urgency and patience, and thus he was used mightily of God to change his family, his Church, and his community for Christ.

If Christians in our own day are similarly going to provoke revival, stability, and justice in this land, they are similarly going to have to reorient themselves to the Biblical perspective of time. If they are going to rebuild the walls of this culture, if they are going to help restore America's greatness, they are going to have to forge a tough balance between urgency and patience.

Urgency without patience is counter productive. It leads to burnout. It creates workaholism. It tends toward wild-eyed fanaticism.

Patience without urgency is counterproductive. It leads to compromise. It creates apathy. It tends toward lackluster sloth-fulness.

The Biblical perspective of time balances urgency with patience. It tames the lion's roar of urgency without defanging it. It invigorates the still water of patience without roiling it.

In the struggle against inhuman humanism's monolithic jug-gernaut, Christians need that kind of balance. They need it des-perately. They need heavy doses of urgency to keep them in the battle lest they tire or bore and head for the refuge of irrele-vance. But, simultaneously, they need heavy doses of patience to keep them on course, steady, and sure, lest they frazzle or frizz and head for the fallow of the fringe.

## Conclusion

The struggle for life, liberty, truth, and righteousness is sure to be a long and tiresome struggle. The humanists have stockpiled an arsenal of resources capable of withstanding a protracted assault. They won't be giving in any time soon. Of that, everyone can be quite certain.

That being the case, Christians are going to have to learn to set a reasonable pace. A pace that keeps both the crises and exigencies of the moment and the assurances and promises of eternity in perspective. A pace that is governed by the Biblical perspective of time.

That perspective, a balance of urgency and patience, is what distinguished the ancient Hebrews and the early Christians from all other peoples. It is what enabled Western Civilization to outstrip all others in progress, change, and development. It is what gave success to the great heroes of the faith throughout all time. It is what gave the Christian missionary movement its irresistible, overwhelming character.

It is what will enable Christians in our own day to affirm with the Psalmist:

> For I hear the slander of many; fear is on every side; while they take counsel together against me, they scheme to take away my life. But as for me, I trust in You, O Lord; I say, "You are my God." My times are in Your hand; deliver me from the hand of my enemies, and from those who persecute me (Psalm 31:13-15).

# ELEVEN

# KEEPING PERSPECTIVE

The campaign had been an emotional roller-coaster. There had been moments of intense and incredible highs. But those had been matched by equally intense and incredible lows.

David Davidson's race for Lieutenant Governor had been fought with difficulty from the start. The naysayers hadn't given him the least bit of a chance: He was a political novice facing the most entrenched and experienced incumbent in the state. He was spurned by his own party because of his explicit and uncompromising Christian stance. He was forced to run the campaign on a fraction of the financial resources of his opponent. And the press utterly ignored his policy proposals and campaign appearances.

Even so, a vast groundswell of grassroots Christian support had buoyed him all along the way to election day.

"The response was remarkable," he said, not long after the campaign had come to an end. "Everywhere we went—and we went *everywhere*—Christians rallied to our cause. They were willing to face the odds. The whole thing was extremely gratifying."

Dollar for dollar, Davidson actually made the best showing of any candidate for statewide office in years. He pulled in new voters. He attracted young and old, conservative and traditionalist, religious and libertarian to the polls. He spawned a massive voter registration drive and an extensive voter education blitz. He stimulated tremendous enthusiasm among various social-issue groups, special-interest groups, pro-life groups, home-school and Christian day-school groups, pro-family advocacy groups, and traditional-morality evangelical groups.

One of the few journalists that did bother to cover the campaign asserted that "if anything can be learned from this, it is this: A little blood, sweat, and tears goes a long, long way in the political process."

And it did go a long, long way. Unfortunately, it didn't go long enough. When the election results were final, Davidson had been trounced. The humanist alliance of Republicans and Democrats was just too much to overcome.

But, though he had lost the election, he was anything but defeated. In the weeks and months following the campaign, Davidson was confidently talking about "next time." Somehow his enthusiasm was unflagging. His determination was undying. His commitment was undaunted.

"The story of this race is still untold," he said. "Because God is in it, my perspective is not controlled by experience or appearance. It is controlled, instead, by the reality of God's promises."

Davidson had an eternal perspective. His work, his sacrifice, and his obedience were not dependent upon instantaneous results. He knew that Scriptural renewal in the political arena might take a very long time and require very strenuous effort. But in the end he knew that it would all be worthwhile because of God's governing hand. He knew that despite temporary setbacks, short-run failures, and minor defeats, the cause of Christ would ultimately triumph. Somehow. Some way.

And with that kind of perspective under his belt, he plunged ahead.

### Very Great and Precious Promises

God promised that His people would be "more than conquerors" (Romans 8:37). He said that they would be "overcomers" (1 John 5:4). And He asserted that they would be victorious in Christ (1 Corinthians 15:57).

The *fact* is, the future belongs to them. The humanist house of cards *will* come tumbling down one day. It is inevitable. It cannot withstand the force of reality.

The *fact* is, Christians are ultimately invincible (Ephesians 6:10-18; Romans 8:37-39). Even the gates of hell cannot prevail against them (Matthew 16:8). All they have to do is go forth with righteousness, steadfastness, and diligence and claim that which is theirs already (Genesis 1:28).

They may have to work with few or even no resources at first. That was certainly the experience of David (1 Samuel 17:38-40) and Jonathan (1 Samuel 14:6). But ultimately Christians will prevail just as David and Jonathan prevailed.

They may have to improvise, laboring under poor conditions, with unqualified workers, and inadequate facilities. That was certainly the experience of Aaron (Exodus 25:1-29) and Nehemiah (Nehemiah 1:20). But ultimately Christians will prevail just as Aaron and Nehemiah prevailed.

They may have to wrestle with the rulers, the powers, and the principalities. That was certainly the experience of Deborah (Judges 4:4-24) and the Apostles (Acts 4:17-20). But ultimately Christians will prevail just as Deborah and the Apostles prevailed.

Instead of allowing their limitations and liabilities to discourage and debilitate them, Christians can tap the eternal wellspring of God's grace and then forge ahead to victory. God's power is thus made manifest in their weaknesses (1 Corinthians 1:26-29).

Instead of bogging down in the exigencies of circumstance, they can rely on God's very great and precious promises (2 Peter 1:3-4).

Thus was Abraham able to obtain victory against the power of Babylon (Genesis 14:13-17). Thus was Moses able to obtain victory against the power of Egypt (Exodus 14:5-31). Thus was Joshua able to obtain victory against the power of Canaan (Joshua 6:1-25). Thus was Ehud able to obtain victory against the power of Moab (Judges 3:12-30), Shamgar against Philistia (Judges 3:31), Gideon against Midian (Judges 6:12-8:35), David against Goliath (1 Samuel 17:42-52), and Jonathan against the Philistines (1 Samuel 14:1-15).

Because of the blessings of the Covenant, God's people are inevitably and inescapably on the winning side of history. History is, after all, His story.

### Bad News and Good News

Even a cursory examination of history demonstrates that God is at work continually redeeming the unredeemable. Every time wickedness, disaster, and crisis emerges in the course of human events, God interrupts the bad news with good news. In fact, history reads like a kind of bad news-good news antiphon.

The bad news: Adam and Eve turned from reliance on God alone and fell into the miserable estate of sin, separation, and depravity.

The good news: God covered their nakedness, provided for their needs, and announced the coming of a Deliverer.

The bad news: The children of Adam and Eve yielded to ever more desperate patterns of rebellion and destruction so that God was compelled to blot out the whole of mankind from the face of the earth with a flood.

The good news: One man found favor with God. Thus, Noah was spared and the race of man was saved from extinction.

The bad news: Almost immediately the sons of Noah began the long, slow downward spiral of reprobation, culminating in the blasphemy of Babel.

The good news: God scattered and confused the infidels, and then called out of the nations a special man to be the father of a special nation to fulfill a special calling in time and eternity.

The bad news: That special man had no natural heirs. He had no son and, thus, no real future.

The good news: God gave Abraham and Sarah a son, through miraculous circumstances, well past the age of child-bearing, thus beginning the Messianic hope.

On and on and on the antiphon goes, throughout the course of history, each new deliverance greater than the one before. Then God played His ultimate good news trump card: the Resurrection of Jesus Christ. Death was swallowed up in victory. Bad news was consumed in good news. The sovereignty of Almighty God in history was made completely and undeniably manifest.

Early in his Presidency, John F. Kennedy asserted that "time is not our friend." But for Christians, that kind of negative resistance to the future is entirely contrary to the facts. The facts are all bound up in the good news of the Gospel. The facts portray the future as a grand dispensation of triumph.

And that's *really* good news.

## Forward Through the Ages

Throughout the history of the Church, faithful disciples have always kept this perspective at the core of their faith and experience. Though they have been tried, imprisoned, persecuted, exiled, scorned, martyred, scourged, maligned, tortured, and deprived, they have always maintained a steadfast trust in their ultimate and consummate victory.

They were stoned, they were sawn in two, were tempted, were slain with the sword. They wandered about in sheepskins and goatskins, being destitute, afflicted, tormented — of whom the world was not worthy. They wandered in deserts and mountains, in dens and caves of the earth (Hebrews 11:37-38).

Yet they never yielded to pessimism or doubt about what God would do. So that, in the end, they did indeed triumph.

Who through faith subdued kingdoms, worked righteousness, obtained promises, stopped the mouths of lions, quenched the violence of fire, escaped the edge of the sword, out of weakness were made strong, became valiant in battle, turned to flight the armies of the aliens (Hebrews 11:33-34).

Such has always been the nature of God's own.

**Augustine of Hippo (354-430) was undeterred in his confidence in God's promised victory.** The great doctor of the early Church ministered from North Africa during a time of great turmoil, upheaval, and unrest. Roman civilization was collapsing in the West. Barbarian invasions into the very heart of the empire had crushed the confidence of the citizenry. Civil instability had broken the efficacy of the economy. And Spiritual tensions had shattered the unity of the Church. Augustine met all these dilemmas and disasters head on with an optimism that utterly unnerved his opponents. His written output was vast: There still survive one hundred thirteen books and treatises, nearly two hundred fifty letters, and more than five hundred sermons. All are infused with the certainty that the cause of truth would prevail. Whether he was writing to answer the Donatist, Manichaean, and Pelagian heresies, or to assure the populace following the Gothic invasion of Rome in 410 or the Vandal invasion of Hippo in 430, he exuded confidence in the very great and precious promises of God. As a result, Augustine had a mighty influence on Christian civilization, paving the way for the great revivals of Calvin, Luther, and the Romanovs.

**Methodius of Salonika (815-885) was undeterred in his confidence in God's promised victory.** After his dramatic conversion he resigned his seat as a provincial governor to join his brother, Cyril, in a pioneer missionary work in Moravia.

God gave them considerable success. They created an alphabet and a written transcription of the Slavic language so that the Bible, Church liturgies, devotional materials, and evangelistic tools could be translated for the use of the common people. They made inroads into virtually all strata of the populace. Revival was everywhere evident. But then controversy broke out. Other missionaries to the region, jealous of Methodius and Cyril's success, began to stir up strife and dissension. The brothers were harassed, persecuted, imprisoned, and exiled. Cyril died prematurely and Methodius was forced to continue the ordeal of tribulation alone. But through it all, he maintained his confidence in the very great and precious promises of God. His vision was fixed on the good news of victory in Christ. His triumphalistic perspective never wavered. As a result, he had a mighty influence over the entire Slavic civilization, a patron to the Czechs, Croats, Serbs, Bulgars, Moravians, and, indeed, all Eastern Europeans.

**Cotton Mather (1663-1727), was undeterred in his confidence in God's promised victory.** A pioneer in the new colonial lands of America, the great Puritan leader forged an exuberant theology of optimism and diligence that would ultimately shape the character of the entire New World culture. The rigors of carving a new life out of the rugged American frontier did not prevent him from writing more than two hundred full-length books and treaties, nearly one thousand sermons, and innumerable letters, articles, and essays. He was actively involved in civic affairs, cultural pursuits, and evangelistic mission. He drew strength for all those activities from the knowledge that God was making the colonies into "a light on a hill, a beacon unto the nations of the glories of our God and King, Jesus." His unremitted confidence in the very great and precious promises of God led him to believe that the "manifest destiny of civilization" lay in this: "that the Christian faith would triumph, that the enemies of Christ would be put asunder, and that the reign of righteousness would usher in from above." He was rooted in a perspective where good news always prevailed over bad news regardless of the circumstances. As a result, he had a mighty influence over the entire American Christian culture, and in fact, over the entire American experience.

Dozens of other Christian stalwarts could be cited, men and women who stood steadfast in the blessed hope of victory of Christ: Jerome of Dalmatia (342-420), Germanus of Constantinople (635-733), John Wyclif (1329-1384), Jan Hus (1374-1415), Demetrius of Rostov (1651-1709), Dwight L. Moody (1837-1899), Nectarius Kephalas (1846-1920), and Francis Schaeffer (1912-1984). Each one of these, and many, many others over the long winding course of time, have demonstrated beyond any shadow of a doubt that the good news of *eternity* can and will be translated into the good news of *history*. By faith through grace.

## Conclusion

God is in control.

History really is His story.

So, victory is imminent. Christians need only to claim it.

If Christians are going to rebuild the walls of this culture, they are going to *have* to claim it. If they are going to help restore America's greatness, they are going to have to maintain the Biblical perspective of triumph that is at the core of the good news.

It would be too easy to become discouraged otherwise. It would be too easy to be overwhelmed. After all, the odds *are* staggering. The issues *are* complex. The opposition *is* monolithic. It would be awfully easy to give up and give in.

Time may be short. Days may be long. And resources may be few. But the victory is assured. There are no ifs, ands, or buts about it.

That being the case, *it's time to go to work*. It's time to rebuild the walls. It's time to restore America's greatness.

Now.

# RESOURCES FOR ACTION

## Books

Athanasius, *On the Incarnation* (Crestwood, New York: St. Vladimir's Seminary Press, 1953).

James H. Billington, *The Icon and the Axe* (New York: Vintage Books, 1966).

Gerald Bray, *Creeds, Councils, and Christ* (Leicester, England: Inter-Varsity Press, 1984).

Lynn Buzzard and Paula Campbell, *Holy Disobedience: When Christians Must Resist the State* (Ann Arbor, Michigan: Servant Books, 1984).

Owen Chadwick, *The Reformation* (Middlesex, England: Penguin Books, 1964).

Oswald Chambers, *My Utmost for His Highest* (New York: Dodd, Mead, and Company, 1935).

David Chilton, *Paradise Restored: An Eschatology of Dominion* (Tyler, Texas: Institute for Christian Economics, 1985).

_____. *Productive Christians in an Age of Guilt-Manipulators*, 3rd rev. ed. (Tyler, Texas: Institute for Christian Economics, 1985).

John Chrysostom, *On Marriage and Family* (Crestwood, New York: St. Vladimir's Seminary Press, 1986).

_____. *On Wealth and Poverty* (Crestwood, New York: St. Vladimir's Seminary Press, 1984).

Gary DeMar, *God and Government: A Biblical and Historical Study* (Atlanta, Georgia: American Vision Press, 1982).

_____. *God and Government: Issues in Biblical Perspective* (Atlanta, Georgia: American Vision Press, 1984).

_____. *God and Government: The Restoration of the Republic* (Atlanta, Georgia: American Vision Press, 1986).

*161*

_____. *Ruler of the Nations: The Biblical Blueprint for Civil Government* (Fort Worth, Texas: Dominion Press, 1987).

Peter E. Gillquist, *Why We Haven't Changed the World* (Old Tappan, New Jersey: Flemming H. Revell, 1982).

George Grant, *Bringing in the Sheaves: Transforming Poverty into Productivity* (Atlanta, Georgia: American Vision Press, 1985).

_____. *The Dispossessed: Homelessness in America* (Westchester, Illinois: Crossway Books, 1986).

_____. *In the Shadow of Plenty: Biblical Principles of Welfare and Poverty* (Nashville, Tennessee: Thomas Nelson, 1986).

_____. *The Changing of the Guard: Biblical Principles for Political Action* (Fort Worth, Texas: Dominion Press, 1987).

_____. *The Big Lie: The Scandal of Planned Parenthood* (Brentwood, Tennessee: Wolgemuth and Hyatt Publishers, 1987).

Thomas Howard, *Evangelical is Not Enough* (Nashville, Tennessee: Thomas Nelson, 1984).

James B. Jordan, *Judges: God's War Against Humanism* (Tyler, Texas: Geneva Ministries, 1985).

_____. *The Law of the Covenant: An Exposition of Exodus 21-23* (Tyler, Texas: Institute for Christian Economics, 1984).

R. B. Kuiper, *The Glorious Body of Christ* (Edinburgh, Scotland: Banner of Truth Trust, 1967).

Tim LaHaye, *Faith of our Founding Fathers* (Brentwood, Tennessee: Wolgemuth and Hyatt Publishers, 1987).

Vishal Mangalwadi, *Truth and Social Reform* (New Delhi, India: Nivedit Books, 1986).

Robert G. Marshall, *Bayonets and Roses: A Comprehensive Pro-Life Political Action Guide* (Falls Church, Virginia: Marshall, 1976).

Gene Newman and Joni Eareckson Tada, *All God's Children: Ministry to the Disabled* (Grand Rapids, Michigan: Zondervan, 1987).

Gary North, *Liberating Planet Earth* (Fort Worth, Texas: Dominion Press, 1987).

Dimitri Obolensky, *The Byzantine Commonwealth* (Crestwood, New York: St. Vladimir's Seminary Press, 1971).

J. I. Packer, *Knowing God* (Downers Grove, Illinois: InterVarsity Press, 1973).

Dennis Peacocke, *Christ the Liberator of the Nations* (Tustin, California: Alive and Free, 1987).

G. L. Prestige, *Fathers and Heretics* (London: SPCK, 1940).

Mary Pride, *The Big Book of Home Learning* (Westchester, Illinois: Crossway Books, 1986).

——————. *The Child Abuse Industry* (Westchester, Illinois: Crossway Books, 1986).

R. J. Rushdoony, *The Institutes of Biblical Law* (Nutley, New Jersey: Craig Press, 1973).

——————. *The Nature of the American System* (Tyler, Texas: Thoburn Press, 1978).

——————. *Politics of Guilt and Pity* (Tyler, Texas: Thoburn Press, 1978).

——————. *This Independent Republic* (Tyler, Texas: Thoburn Press, 1978).

Francis Schaeffer, *A Christian Manifesto* (Westchester, Illinois: Crossway Books, 1981).

——————. *How Should We Then Live* (Old Tappan, New Jersey: Fleming H. Revell, 1976).

——————. *Two Contents, Two Realities* (Downers Grove, Illinois: InterVarsity Press, 1974).

Philip Schaff, *The Principle of Protestantism* (Boston: United Church Press, 1964).

Phyllis Schlafly ed., *Child Abuse in the Classroom* (Westchester, Illinois: Crossway Books, 1984).

Ray Sutton, *That You May Prosper: Dominion By Covenant* (Fort Worth, Texas: Dominion Press, 1987).

Thomas J. Talley, *The Origins of the Liturgical Year* (New York: Pueblo Publishing Co., 1986).

Robert Thoburn, *The Christian and Politics* (Tyler, Texas: Thoburn Press, 1984).

Henry Van Til, *The Calvinistic Concept of Culture* (Philadelphia: Presbyterian and Reformed, 1959).

Rus Walton, *One Nation Under God* (Nashville, Tennessee: Thomas Nelson, 1987).

John W. Whitehead, *An American Dream* (Westchester, Illinois: Crossway Books, 1987).

E. C. Wines, *The Hebrew Republic* (Uxbridge, Massachusetts: American Presbyterian Press, 1980).

## Book Services

American Vision, P.O. Box 720515, Atlanta, Georgia, 30328.

Christian Worldview Book Service, P.O. Box 1141, Humble, Texas, 77347.

Fairfax Christian Books, P.O. Box 6941, Tyler, Texas, 75711.

Government Printing Office, Washington, D.C., 20402.

Powerful Living, P.O. Box 8204, Fort Worth, Texas, 76124.

Puritan and Reformed Discount Books, 1319 Newport Gap Pike, Wilmington, Delaware, 19804.

Ross House Books, P.O. Box 67, Vallecito, California, 95251.

Trinity Book Service, P.O. Box 131300, Tyler, Texas, 75713.

## Radio Broadcasts

*The Cal Thomas Report*, 11422 Huntsman, Manassas, Virginia, 22111.

*The Christian Worldview*, P.O. Box 1144, Brentwood, Tennessee, 37027.

*Contact America*, 717 Second Street N.E., Washington, D.C., 20002.

*Focus on the Family*, 41 E. Foothill Blvd., Arcadia, California, 91006.

*Good News Communications*, 2876 Mabry N.E., Atlanta, Georgia, 30319.

*Point of View*, P.O. Box 30, Dallas, Texas, 75221.

## Newsletters

*American Vision*, P.O. Box 720515, Atlanta, Georgia, 30328.

*Chalcedon Report*, P.O. Box 158, Vallecito, California, 95251.

*Christian Worldview*, P.O. Box 1144, Brentwood, Tennessee, 37027.

*ClipNotes*, P.O. Box 8204, Fort Worth, Texas, 76124.

*Coalition of Unregistered Churches*, 2560 Sylvan Road, East Point, Georgia, 30344.

*Geneva Review*, P.O. Box 131300, Tyler, Texas, 75713.

*Good News Communications*, 2876 Mabry Road N.E., Atlanta, Georgia, 30319.

*Forerunner*, P.O. Box 1799, Gainesville, Florida, 31602.

*Intercessors for America*, P.O. Box 2639, Reston, Virginia, 22090.

*Institute for Christian Economics*, P.O. Box 8000, Tyler, Texas, 75701.

*Plymouth Rock Foundation*, P.O. Box 425, Marlborough, New Hampshire, 03455.

*Remnant Review*, P.O. Box 8204, Fort Worth, Texas, 76124.

*Rescue*, P.O. Box 1141, Humble, Texas, 77347.

*Rutherford Institute Report*, P.O. Box 5101, Manassas, Virginia, 22110.

*Texas Christian Heritage Foundation*, P.O. Box 162726, Austin, Texas, 78716.

*Texas Grassroots Coalition*, 95001 Capitol of Texas North, #304, Austin, Texas, 78759.

*To the Work*, P.O. Box 1144, Brentwood, Tennessee, 37027.

*Vorthos*, P.O. Box 1144, Brentwood, Tennessee, 37027

*Washington Report*, P.O. Box 8204, Fort Worth, Texas, 76124.

*Public Eye*, P.O. Box 26010, Philadelphia, Pennsylvania, 19128.

## Magazines and Journals

*Candidates Biblical Scoreboard*, P.O. Box 10428, Costa Mesa, California, 92627.

*Christianity and Civilization*, P.O. Box 131300, Tyler, Texas, 75713.

*Chronicles of Culture*, 934 Main Street, Rockford, Illinois, 61103.

*Communication Institute*, P.O. Box 612, Champaign, Illinois, 61820.

*Congressional Quarterly Weekly Report*, NAE Office of Public Affairs, 1430 K Street N.W., Washington, D.C., 20005.

*Counsel of Chalcedon*, P.O. Box 888022, Atlanta, Georgia, 30338.

*Conservative Digest*, P.O. Box 2246, Fort Collins, Colorado, 80522.

*Focus on the Family*, 41 E. Foothill Blvd., Arcadia, California, 91006.

*How to Become an Effective Grassroot Lobbyist*, Free Congress Research and Education Foundation, 721 Second Street N.E., Washington, D.C., 20002.

*Human Life Review*, 150 E. 35th Street, #840, New York, New York, 10016.

*Insight*, 3600 New York Avenue N.E., Washington, D.C., 20002.

*National Prayer Committee*, P.O. Box 6826, San Bernadino, California, 92412.

*New American*, 395 Concord Avenue, Belmont, Massachusetts, 02178.

*The World and I*, 2850 New York Avenue N.E., Washington, D.C., 20077.

*This World*, P.O. Box 26010, Philadelphia, Pennsylvania, 19128.

## Tape Services

Chalcedon Audio-Visual Productions, P.O. Box 158, Vallecito, California, 95251.

Firestorm Chats, P.O. Box 8204, Fort Worth, Texas, 76124.

Geneva Ministries, P.O. Box 131300, Tyler, Texas, 75713.

L'Abri Cassettes, P.O. Box 2035, Michigan City, Indiana, 46360.

Vorthos Tapes, P.O. Box 1141, Humble, Texas, 77347.

## Correspondence

A Letterwriter's Guide to Congress, Chamber of Commerce of the United States, 1615 H. Street N.W., Washington, D.C., 20062.

*Congressional Record*, Superintendent of Documents, U.S. Government Printing Office, Washington, D.C., 20402; 202-783-3238.

Legislative Information Office, 202-225-1772 from 7 A.M. to 11 P.M. EST., seven days a week.

U.S. Capitol Switchboard, 202-225-1771 from 7 A.M. to 11 P.M. EST., seven days a week.

White House Comment Line: 202-456-7639, Justice Department Busing Complaint Line: 202-633-3847, General Litigation Complaint Line: 202-633-4713.

*A Congressional Staff Directory* may be purchased at a cost of $25.00 prepaid from Congressional Staff Directory, P.O. Box 62, Mount Vernon, Virginia, 22121.

For $2.00 you can send a fifteen word message (a personal opinion wire) to any legislator. The bill will be sent to you or put on your phone bill. Call your Western Union office.

One of the many groups publishing voting records of Congressmen is the Committee for the Survival of a Free Congress, 721 2nd Street N.E., Washington, D.C., 20002.

To listen to recorded messages on the latest legislative activity, call 202-224-8541 (for Senate Democrats); 202-244-8601 (for Senate Republicans); 202-225-7400 (for House Democrats); and 202-225-7430 (for House Republicans).

## Computer Services

*American Press International*, P.O. Box 2246, Fort Collins, Colorado, 80522.

*Contact America Network*, 717 Second Street N.E., Washington, D.C., 20002.

*POLSYS*, P.O. Box 281, Falls Church, Virginia, 22042.

# COLOPHON

The typeface for the text of this book is *Baskerville*. Its creator, John Baskerville (1706-1775), broke with tradition to reflect in his type the rounder, yet more sharply cut lettering of eighteenth-century stone inscriptions and copy books. The type foreshadows modern design in such novel characteristics as the increase in contrast between thick and thin strokes and the shifting of stress from the diagonal to the vertical strokes. Realizing that this new style of letter would be most effective if cleanly printed on smooth paper with genuinely black ink, he built his own presses, developed a method of hot-pressing the printed sheet to a smooth, glossy finish, and experimented with special inks. However, Baskerville did not enter into general commercial use in England until 1923.

Substantive editing by Michael S. Hyatt
Copy editing by James B. Jordan
Cover design by Kent Puckett Associates, Atlanta, Georgia
Typography by Thoburn Press, Tyler, Texas
Printed and bound by Arcata Graphics, Fairfield, Pennsylvania